L
T

Int
Lis

Prev

Clare West

CAMBRIDGE
UNIVERSITY PRESS

University Printing House, Cambridge CB2 8BS, United Kingdom

Cambridge University Press is part of the University of Cambridge.

It furthers the University's mission by disseminating knowledge in the pursuit of education, learning and research at the highest international levels of excellence.

www.cambridge.org
Information on this title: www.cambridge.org/9780521140348 (without key)
www.cambridge.org/9780521140362 (with key)

© Clare West 1999

First published by Georgian Press (Jersey) Limited 1999
Reprinted and published by Cambridge University Press 2010
5th printing 2013

A catalogue record for this publication is available from the British Library

ISBN 978-0-521-14034-8 Paperback without key
ISBN 978-0-521-14036-2 Paperback with key

Produced by AMR Design Ltd (www.amrdesign.com)
Drawings by David Birdsall, Tony Jones and Rania Varvaki
Cover image: © Shutterstock

CONTENTS

The Tapescripts begin on page 65 of the With Key edition.
The Key begins on page 88 of the With Key edition.

INTRODUCTION

Listen Here! is for students at lower intermediate to intermediate level who want to improve their listening in English. It also offers useful practice to those preparing for the Cambridge Preliminary English Test (PET). It can be used to supplement any coursebook at this level, and is suitable for use in the classroom, or in the case of the With Key edition, for self-study.

Listen Here! provides:

- over 2½ hours of recorded material on two C80 cassettes
- lively recordings in standard and regional British English
- occasional American and Australian voices
- a wide range of topics taken from the PET syllabus
- a variety of tasks for active listening
- additional speaking and pronunciation practice
- a simple, attractive layout, so that the material is easy to use.

How is the book organised?

There are 28 double-page topic-based units. Each unit consists of two recorded texts with a number of activities, a pronunciation or speaking exercise, and sometimes a listening tip. The Tapescripts and the Key are at the end of the With Key edition.

There is an index to the Pronunciation and Speaking exercises, and also a Pronunciation Bank to help students with unusual or difficult words, especially place names.

How should Listen Here! be used?

Teachers using the book as supplementary material should feel free to dip in and out of the units as they wish. However, the units are graded in order of difficulty, starting with the easiest, so students studying on their own should work through the units in order. Later units have more difficult texts, or more difficult tasks. A gradual approach will help to build up skills and confidence.

Tips for the teacher

This book aims to reflect what happens in the classroom and real life, by adopting an integrated approach to the skills of listening and speaking. A purely listening lesson may become stressful and tense, with the whole class listening silently, nervously and unprepared for the correct answer. Instead, communicative activities can be used to introduce the topic orally, which will help to put students in the most receptive mood for listening, and feedback can be lively and enjoyable.

Choose units that you feel are appropriate for your class's listening level and general interests. Use Part A as a warm-up or to predict or present vocabulary or ideas that will be needed in the rest of the unit. Then move on to Part B. Allow students time to look at the rubric first, and then play the recording as often as necessary. You will have to rewind the tape, as each recording appears only once (except in the Pronunciation exercises in Part D).

Encourage plenty of feedback and discussion in pairs or small groups and the whole class, before moving on to Part C. In most units this involves a new recording and new tasks, still on the same theme. Leave a little time at the end of the lesson for the Speaking or Pronunciation activities (Part D in most units). Many teachers find that a brief but regular focus on stress, intonation and pronunciation is the best way to improve students' ability to make themselves understood, as well as their ability to understand other people.

Tips for the student

- Start with Unit 1, or choose another unit in the first five if you prefer. Look at the title, and think about the topic for a few minutes (in English!).

- Work through the unit, listening to the tape as often as you like. You will have to rewind the tape each time you want to listen to a recording again (except in Part D).

- If you are alone, practise the speaking exercises by speaking aloud to yourself. Practise the pronunciation exercises in front of a mirror, so that you can see exactly how your mouth and lips are moving.

- Don't forget to read and think about the Listening Tips at the end of some units. You may find the Pronunciation Bank at the end of the book useful, too.

- The more often you listen to a recording, the more you will understand, so listen to it on your walkman, in your car or at home, if you can.

Finally ...

I hope you all enjoy using *Listen Here!*

CLARE WEST

This book is dedicated to my daughter Leila.

1 FACTS AND FIGURES

A

Do you find it easier to remember facts or figures? Look at this box for 30 seconds and memorise as much as you can.

The capital of Australia is Canberra.	23 September 1913
The Globe Theatre was burned down in 1613.	4879133
Red hair is stronger than blond hair.	01772 651504

Close your book and write down what you remember, or tell your partner. If numbers are more difficult for you, can you think of any ways of making them easier to remember?

B1

A teacher wants to arrange accommodation for a group of students on a farm. Listen to his phone conversation and tick (✔) the correct sentences.

1 The teacher has a small group of students.
2 Accommodation at Mill House Barns is cheap.
3 Bathrooms and hot water are available.
4 The students are used to better living conditions.
5 Everything is provided.
6 The students are going to stay there for four nights.
7 It is necessary to pay in advance.
8 The teacher is pleased with the arrangement.

B2

Listen again and complete the teacher's notes.

Mill House Farm   Owner: _____
No. of students _____
Cost per student _____
What about beds? _____
   "   washing facilities? _____
   "   food?   Do own cooking
Students must bring with them _____
No. of nights _____
Dates _____
Time of arrival _____
Total cost _____
How to pay? _____
When? _____

C1

Listen to the conversation about general knowledge and circle the correct answers (A, B or C).

1 Who was the first man on the moon?
A Yuri Gagarin
B Buzz Aldrin
C Neil Armstrong

2 Which country has the most TV sets?
A USA
B China
C Japan

3 What's the most expensive film ever made?
A *Gone with the Wind*
B *Jurassic Park*
C *Titanic*

4 Who sailed across the Pacific on a raft?
A Francis Chichester
B Thor Heyerdahl
C Robert Scott

5 How many hairs are there on the average human head?
A 1,000,000
B 1,000   C 100,000

6 Who was the youngest ever Wimbledon tennis champion?
A Martina Hingis
B Boris Becker
C Michael Chang

C2

Listen to these phrases from the recording and choose the correct words or phrases you hear from the pairs in the box.

1 haven't ever / haven't even
2 we only need about / we only need a boat
3 shall we start / should we start
4 who first stepped / who first tapped
5 wouldn't they / mightn't they
6 no, my dear / no idea
7 actually / really
8 on a raft / on or after
9 a member – him / remember him
10 I should say / I should think

D

PRONUNCIATION PRACTICE: Dates and numbers

Listen and repeat these dates and numbers after the speaker.

6 AD   1066   1872   1901   1924   the year 2000
25th May   14th February   December 11th   1st June   3rd March
1,000,000   100,000   1,000   1,001   132   89
13 30   15 50   17 70   18 80   19 90
557216   643801   9473862   525813   296017   (telephone numbers)

Listening tip Listen extra carefully to numbers, dates and names. Always check if you aren't sure, for example: 'Sorry, was that 16 or 60?' 'Did you say June or July?' 'Do you spell it with an i or not?' 'Is it 772138 or 772148?'

2 HAVING FUN

A

Which activity in these pictures would you prefer, and why?

A   B   C

B1

When **Ted** comes home, he finds three recorded messages on his answerphone. Read the sentences, then listen and choose from **A, B** or **C** to complete the sentences correctly.

1 The messages are all   A invitations   B complaints   C instructions.
2 Ted is   A a film student   B a dancer   C a manager.
3 Donald Ferguson is   A Ted's friend   B Ted's boss   C Ted's neighbour.
4 Carol is   A Ted's girlfriend   B Ted's wife   C Ted's sister.
5 The times mentioned are   A mostly for this week   B only for this week
   C mostly for next week.

B2

Listen again and complete the information in Ted's notebook.

1 From: _____	When: _____	
About: seeing a film	What time: _____	
Where: the Odeon	Where to meet: _____	
2 From: Donald Ferguson	When: _____	
About: _____	What time: _____	
Where: _____	Dress: not formal	
3 From: Jason	When: _____	
About: _____	What time: _____	
Where: his place	Address: _____	

MESSAGES

C1

Listen to two people, Sophie and Sally, arranging a party. Read the questions, then listen and choose the correct answer (A, B or C).

1 Who is leaving?   A Thomas   B Trevor   C Terry
2 Who is going to book the restaurant?   A Sally   B Sophie   C Susie
3 Which restaurant is it?   A Othello   B Otello's   C O'Dells
4 How many people will be at the dinner?   A 50   B 15   C 55
5 What time will the booking be for?   A 7.00   B 7.15   C 7.30
6 How long has Trevor worked for the company?   A 14 years   B 10 years   C 4 years
7 What extra thing should the restaurant provide?   A a cake   B a special dish
    C a plate with his name on
8 What are they thinking of doing after the dinner?   A going home   B singing
    C dancing

C2

Listen again and find the exact words which are used instead of the phrases or sentences below.

1 In two weeks' time.
2 I'll do it immediately.
3 I hope they aren't fully booked.
4 How long has he worked here?
5 We'll give him a good farewell party.
6 I like the sound of that!

D

PRONUNCIATION PRACTICE: Word and sentence stress

Listen to these sentences and underline wherever you hear a strong stress. Number 1 is done as an example.

1 I'll <u>see</u> you to<u>mo</u>rrow.
2 She posted the letter last night.
3 The present? Oh, give it to him!
4 The piano was sold for a hundred pounds.
5 When does the bank close?
6 He'll set the table for you.
7 I bought a really beautiful jacket there.
8 Sit down and have a cup of coffee.

Listen again, and repeat after the speaker.

Listening tip
If you have difficulty breaking English up into groups of words you can recognise, listen for stress, which is usually on nouns and verbs. Many of the unstressed sounds are not important for general understanding.

3 SOUNDS DELICIOUS!

A   **Think about or discuss these questions about food.**

What kind of food do you like? Is there any food you dislike?
Do you eat meat, or are you a vegetarian?
Do you eat just one big meal a day, or several small meals or snacks?
Do you sometimes go out to eat? What types of restaurant do you like?
Can you cook? What are your specialities?

B1   **You are going to hear somebody giving a friend a recipe for making soup.**
Listen and tick (✔) the types of food that you hear.

apple	carrots	cucumber	milk	potatoes
beef	cheese	lemon	mushroom	salmon
bread	chicken	lettuce	oil	tomatoes
butter	courgettes	melon	onions	yogurt

Ask your teacher or use a picture dictionary to find the meanings of words you don't know.

B2   **The sentences in this recipe are in the wrong order. Listen again and put them in the**
correct order.

A   Fry the chicken in oil or butter
B   Stir the food with a wooden spoon.
C   Add cheese or yogurt, if you like.
D   Add the vegetables to the chicken.
E   Cut up the chicken.
F   Bring the mixture to the boil.
G   Chop the vegetables into small pieces.
H   Put in some pepper and salt.
I   Add half a litre of water to the pan.
J   Fry the chicken and vegetables together.

Does it sound like a good recipe? Could *you* cook this dish? Would you like to?
Why or why not?

C1 You are going to hear somebody ordering a meal in a restaurant. Listen and write down the names of any food or drink you hear.

```
┌─────────────────────────────────────────────────────────────────┐
│                                                                   │
│                                                                   │
│                                                                   │
│                                                                   │
│                                                                   │
│                                                                   │
└─────────────────────────────────────────────────────────────────┘
```

C2 Listen again and fill in the gaps in the conversation.

WAITER: Would you like to (1) _____ now, madam?

CUSTOMER: Yes, I think I'll have the cream of mushroom (2) _____ to start with,

(3) _____.

WAITER: Cream of (4) _____, right.

CUSTOMER: Then I'll have a green (5) _____, with a (6) _____, I think.

WAITER: (7) _____ do you like it done, madam?

CUSTOMER: Oh, (8) _____, thank you.

WAITER: With chips or new (9) _____?

CUSTOMER: Chips, please. And I'll have the (10) _____ pudding – no, on second

thoughts, the (11) _____ fruit salad afterwards. It's (12) _____!

WAITER: Yes, quite! Now, anything to (13) _____? Some wine, perhaps?

CUSTOMER: No, just a bottle of (14) _____ water, I think.

WAITER: Thank you, madam. And for you, sir?

D **SPEAKING PRACTICE**

1 Imagine you're in a café, snack bar or restaurant. What would you like to eat? Give your order to the waiter or waitress. With a partner, take turns to be the customer and the waiter.

2 Ask your partner, *'What's your favourite dish in your country? Can you tell me how to make it?'* He or she can ask you, too.

Listening tip Remember, it isn't always necessary to understand every word when you're listening, so don't panic. Don't think about the words you didn't understand the first time. Relax, and listen again.

4 TICKETS PLEASE!

A

Think about or discuss these questions about travel.

How often do you travel by train or bus? Do you travel by public transport
a) to go to school or work?   b) on weekend excursions to visit friends or family?
c) when you go on holiday?   d) to go shopping?
Do you prefer travelling by car? Is it cheaper or more convenient than using public transport in
your country?

B1

You are planning to make a train journey soon. You know the route (Gatwick to London), but you would like to make sure there have been no recent changes to the timetable. Listen to the recorded announcement and decide which number you should choose for the information you want.

Number _____

B2

Listen again and fill in the missing information.

Thank you for calling Connex (1) _____ (2) _____.

For general information on (3) _____ availability and fares, please (4) _____

National Rail Enquiries on (5) _____.

Please make (6) _____ selection from the (7) _____ numbers.

Press 1 for a recorded (8) _____ on all Connex trains (9) _____ London.

Press 2 if you have any (10) _____ on the way in (11) _____ we could

improve our (12) _____.

Press 3 if you (13) _____ to purchase or (14) _____ a season ticket by

(15) _____ card.

Press 4 for (16) _____ other information or if you would like to be

(17) _____ to one of our (18) _____ advisers.

Please (19) _____ the number you (20) _____ now.

What happens in your country? Do you phone the station, or a central number, if you want
information on trains? Or do you have your own train timetable at home? Can you look up
the train timetable on a computer?

What do you think is the best way of finding out this sort of information?

C1

You are going to hear another recorded message, this time for a national coach company. Read the questions, then listen and answer them.

1 Which towns are mentioned?
2 What are the coach stations called?
3 How long does the coach journey between the two places usually take?
4 Does Saturday count as part of the weekend?
5 What is the cheapest possible fare?
6 What number do you phone to book a ticket?

C2

Look at the timetable first. Then listen again and fill in the gaps.

NATIONAL EXPRESS COACHES Monday to Friday		
BRIGHTON	**LONDON**	**BRIGHTON**
Dep 06.00	Arr _____	
Dep _____	Arr 08.40	
	Dep 08.45	Arr _____
Dep _____	Arr 10.40	
Dep every hour on the hour from _____	Arr _____ later	
	Dep every hour on the _____ from 09.30	Arr 1 hour 50 mins later
Saturday and Sunday		
Dep _____	Arr 08.10	
Dep every hour on the hour from _____	Arr 1 hour 50 mins later	
	Dep every hour on the half hour from 10.30	Arr 1 hour 50 mins later
Fares		
Single	Return	Day return
Adult: £6	£_____	£8
Student: £_____	£7.50	£6
Child: £_____	£5	£4
(Child=under 14 Dep=Departs Arr=Arrives)		

D

SPEAKING PRACTICE

Imagine you are at a railway or bus station ticket office. You want to buy a ticket. Practise your conversation with a partner, using the following conversation to help you.

A: *Hello, I'd like a single/return/day return to Glasgow/London/Manchester, please.*
B: *Right, what time are you travelling?*
A: *I'm going on the 3.20/4.45/7.32/1.54 in ten minutes' time.*
B: *OK, that'll be £5.60/£27.80/£94.63/£13.15, please.*
A: *Here's my Visa card. Can I have a receipt please?*
B: *Right you are. Sign here, please. There's your card and receipt, and your ticket.*
A: *Thank you. Which platform is it?*
B: *Platform number 3/4/5/6/7/8, up the stairs and over the bridge.*
A: *Thanks a lot. Goodbye.*

5 TAKE A MESSAGE

A If you come home and find a message from any of these people on your answerphone, what do you expect to hear? Write down two or three phrases the messages might contain.

1 from a local charity _____

2 from your boss _____

3 from your parents _____

4 from a friend _____

5 from the secretary of a local sports club _____

6 from your doctor's receptionist _____

B1 You are going to hear some messages people left on Sylvia's answerphone while she was away one weekend. Listen and complete the information on Sylvia's notepad.

1 From: Mr Ian Rogers
  About: _____
  Action to take: ring him to explain
  Number: _____

○ 2 From: Mum
  About: checking on Sylvia's health
  Action to take: _____
  Number (mobile): _____

3 From: _____
  About: arriving late at work and leaving early
  Action to take: _____

○ 4 From: _____
  About: charity work
  Action to take: ring him back if interested
  Number: _____

B2 Listen again and answer the questions.

1 When was Sylvia's appointment?
2 What will happen if she doesn't ring Mr Rogers?
3 Why is Sylvia's mother especially worried about her?
4 Why is Jenny Smith, Sylvia's boss, ringing her at home?
5 Which charity does Edward Fowles work for?
6 Which activities would he like Sylvia to help with?

C1
You are working for a language school one summer, and are helping out at reception. The first thing to do when you arrive at work on Monday morning is to listen to all the messages on the answerphone. Listen and decide whether the statements are true (T) or false (F).

1 Guy Bannister is one of the teachers at the school.
2 He has a visa problem in Moscow.
3 He is arriving on Tuesday.
4 Susanna Fernandez's students have already booked their language course.
5 Her students want to stay for ten weeks.
6 Margareta Svensson is going to miss the first week of her course.
7 She cannot attend because her family are very ill.
8 Barry's car crashed into the school minibus.
9 Fortunately, the minibus is not badly damaged.

C2
Listen again and say how the people giving the messages feel. Choose from the words in the box to describe their feelings.

impatient	very worried	relaxed	sorry	angry

1 Guy _____

2 Susanna _____

3 Margareta _____

4 Barry _____

D

SPEAKING PRACTICE

Write down your own message to a friend, and think what you would say if his/her answerphone is switched on. Make sure you give your name and phone number, and a very clear message. And keep it short! Now say your message to a partner, and ask if the message was clear. Practise again.

Listening tip
Be prepared. Try to think what topics and vocabulary the listening will be about. Before you listen to a recorded message or an answerphone, take a few moments to go through useful vocabulary in your mind. For example, before listening to the answerphone at a language school, you might think of *flight, students, visa, agent, teacher, intensive course, family,* etc. This will help you to understand the message better.

6 THE MISSING DIAMONDS

A

Here are some useful words for talking about a crime. Do you know what they mean? Can you add any more words to the list?

motive	suspect	investigate
opportunity	alibi	solve
clues	innocent	solution
evidence	guilty	

B

Read the following information carefully.

Lady Paula Prendergast was giving one of her famous dinner parties at her beautiful country house, Pringle Hall. Several close friends were staying there, including her ex-husband Sir Montague Wilberforce, her future husband Derek Donovan, the actor, and Lucy Bisto, a friend of the Honourable Charles Wilberforce, Lady Paula's son. Morgan the butler and Mrs Forbes the housekeeper were also in the house at the time. Suddenly, in the middle of dinner, Lady Paula put her hands to her neck and cried out in horror, 'My diamonds! Where are they? My diamond necklace is missing!' The dinner was left half eaten on the table, as everybody started searching the house for the necklace, but there was no sign of it. It became clear that the necklace, which was worth about half a million pounds, had been lying on the dressing-table in Lady Paula's bedroom between 6 and 7pm. Lady Paula could not remember putting it on for dinner, so it seemed probable that someone had taken it from her bedroom.

B1

Listen to the conversation between the Honourable Charles and Lucy Bisto. Where was everyone between 6 and 7pm? Write each person's name in the correct room, and what he/she was doing.

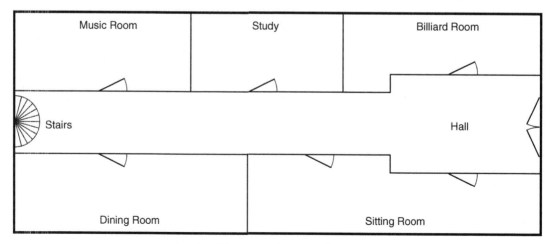

PRINGLE HALL: GROUND FLOOR

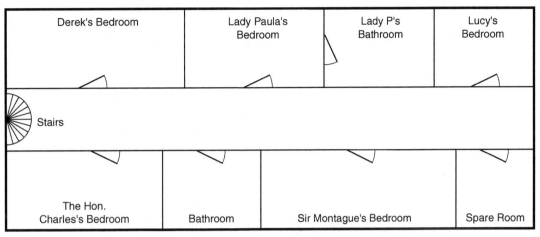

PRINGLE HALL: FIRST FLOOR

Who do you think had *the best opportunity* of stealing the diamonds? Discuss your answers with a partner.

B2 **Now listen to the conversation between Morgan and Mrs Forbes and answer the questions.**

1 Why does Derek want to marry Lady Paula?
2 What does Morgan the butler think about Lady Paula's future marriage to Derek?
3 How does Sir Montague feel about his divorce from Lady Paula?
4 What are his feelings towards Derek Donovan?
5 Why does Lucy hate Lady Paula?
6 Why does Charles need money?
7 What is Mrs Forbes' personal problem?
8 Who do you think has *the best motive* for stealing the diamonds?

Discuss your answers with a partner, and decide who you think the thief was.

Now tell the rest of the class. Be prepared to give your reasons.

C **PRONUNCIATION PRACTICE:** /ɒ/ /ʌ/ and /e/ /æ/

Watch out for differences in the pronunciation of short vowels. Listen and repeat these words and sentences after the speaker.

1 cot, cut   got, gut   gone, gun   shot, shut   cop, cup   not, nut   choc, chuck

Have a cup of coffee? With some nuts, or some chocolate?
Bob lost his job and had to cut his costs.
Tom shut up shop and chucked the key in a bucket.
He's got a lot of bottle, but the cops have gone for him with their guns!

2 pet, pat   men, man   Ben, ban   letter, latter   said, sad   met, mat   pen, pan

The men banned Pat from using her pen.
The cat sat on the mat and Ben penned a letter.
Ben patted his pet and said sadly, 'I've never met a cat like you!'

7 STAYING HEALTHY

A

Look at the pictures. Which activities are good for you? Which do you think could be bad for your health?

B1

You are going to hear five young people talking about exercise, fitness and general health. Listen and match the speakers 1–5 to the pictures above. There is one extra picture.

B2

Read the statements, then listen again and choose one correct statement for each speaker. There are two extra statements.

Speaker 1	A ... has tried to give something up.
Speaker 2	B ... hates exercise.
Speaker 3	C ... plays and watches a sport.
Speaker 4	D ... takes exercise every day.
Speaker 5	E ... is fitter now than last year.
	F ... only exercises at weekends.
	G ... enjoys exercising with friends.

Why do people take exercise?
What kind of exercise do you take, and how often? Do you think you should take more, or less?
What is the best kind of exercise, do you think?
What kind of foods are good or bad for you? Make a list, and see if other students agree with you.

C1 You are going to hear a doctor talking on a radio programme. She is giving some advice on staying fit and healthy. Look at the words in the box, then listen and tick (✔) the ones that you hear.

bread	energy	meals	tennis
cheese	exercise	salt	vegetables
coffee	football	stress	vitamins
diet	fruit	tea	wine

C2 Listen again and tick (✔) the correct sentences.

1 Breakfast is not an important meal.
2 We should eat a large lunch.
3 It's necessary to put a little salt in food while it is cooking.
4 Drink as much tea and coffee as you like.
5 We should eat different kinds of food.
6 Everybody needs the same amount of exercise.
7 Aerobics is a better type of exercise than swimming.
8 It's important to choose a type of exercise that you like.
9 You can save money by taking exercise.
10 You can phone Dr O'Neill tomorrow to ask about stress.

D SPEAKING PRACTICE

Do you agree with Dr O'Neill's ideas?
How do *you* keep fit?
How often are you ill?
How much exercise do you take every week?
How much water do you drink every day?

Find out what other students' answers to these questions are.

Listening tip Don't be afraid to ask the speaker to repeat or explain what s/he said, as Ryan did in the interview. If you don't understand when you're listening, say:
I'm sorry, I didn't quite catch what you said about ...
Sorry to interrupt, but ...
Could I just ask ...
Did you say ... or ...?
Sorry, what was that?
What did you say your name was?
Sorry?   Pardon?
Make sure your voice goes up at the end of your question.

8 HOW DO YOU SAY...?

A

When speaking or writing to people we don't know well, we usually use formal language. With other people, we use informal language. Decide whether these expressions are formal (F) or informal (I).

Sorry I forgot ...	*Please accept this.*
I am extremely grateful.	*I hope that you have an enjoyable time.*
Bye, see you later.	*Have fun!*
I do apologise.	*Thanks a lot.*
Here, take this.	*How do you do?*
Hi there!	*My regards to your parents. Goodbye.*

Now find expressions from the list above (one formal and one informal) which have a similar meaning, to make six pairs.

B1

You are going to hear five speakers, using formal and informal language. Read the statements, then listen and choose the correct statement for each speaker. There are three extra statements.

Speaker 1	A	... is leaving his/her job.
Speaker 2	B	... has photocopied the wrong report.
Speaker 3	C	... has forgotten to book some tickets.
Speaker 4	D	... is asking for advice.
Speaker 5	E	... is giving a talk.
	F	... wants to change some concert tickets.
	G	... thinks someone isn't doing his/her job properly.
	H	... has not met this person before.

B2

Listen to the tone of voice this time, as well as the words, and match each speaker to the correct feeling. There are three extra feelings.

Speaker 1	A	bored
Speaker 2	B	miserable
Speaker 3	C	angry
Speaker 4	D	tired
Speaker 5	E	pleased
	F	grateful
	G	sorry
	H	hopeful

C1 You are going to hear a student talking about the languages that he speaks. Listen and tick (✔) the correct information.

1 Fluent languages: Malay Chinese Arabic English German

2 Father's nationality: English German Chinese Malaysian

3 Mother's nationality: Chinese Italian English Egyptian

4 Speaks a little: German Italian English Arabic

5 Best at speaking: English Arabic Malay Chinese

6 Best at writing: Arabic English German Chinese Malay

7 Wants to improve: Chinese English German Arabic

C2 Listen again and match the two halves of the sentences.

1 He speaks Malay
2 He speaks Mandarin Chinese
3 He speaks English
4 He lives in Kuala Lumpur,
5 He speaks Chinese with his friends,
6 His main problem is listening,
7 He'd like to travel abroad

A which is the capital of Malaysia.
B because he was sent to an English school.
C to improve his languages.
D because his father's Malaysian.
E because his mother's Chinese.
F so that's his favourite language.
G because people speak so fast.

D PRONUNCIATION PRACTICE: Contractions

We often run words together, or shorten them, so it's sometimes difficult to hear all the words in a sentence. Listen to the six sentences and write down the number of words in them. A contraction (like *I've, he's, isn't*) counts as two words.

1 ____   2 ____   3 ____   4 ____   5 ____   6 ____

Listen and repeat these forms after the speaker:

she's   I've   haven't   isn't   we're   here's   you'll

Listen to the six sentences again and repeat after the speaker.

Listening tip English sounds in slow, formal speech may sound quite different in informal conversations, or when people speak fast. Look out for these contractions:

I'd (= I had/ I would)   *he's* (= he has/he is)
isn't (= is not)   *doesn't* (= does not)
can't (= cannot)   *aren't* (= are not)
won't (= will not)   *shan't* (= shall not)

9 FLYING HIGH

What is happening in the picture? What words or phrases do you hear or use when talking about flights? Match the questions to the answers.

1 *Which gate number is it?*
2 *How early do we have to check in?*
3 *Is it a scheduled or charter flight?*
4 *How much hand luggage can I take with me?*
5 *Is there a reduction for children?*
6 *Can I have a window seat?*

A *Only one bag, I'm afraid.*
B *Scheduled – it goes daily.*
C *Yes, 50%.*
D *Number 24.*
E *Sorry, they've all been taken.*
F *Two hours before departure.*

Which of questions 1–6 are probably asked at the travel agent's, and which at the airport check-in desk?

B1

You are going to hear four people asking for or giving information about flying. Read the statements, then listen and choose the correct statement for each speaker. There are two extra statements.

Speaker 1
Speaker 2
Speaker 3
Speaker 4

A ... is checking in at the airport.
B ... is making a complaint.
C ... is asking for information.

D ... is confirming flight details.
E ... is changing a flight.
F ... is booking a flight.

B2

Read the statements, then listen again and decide whether they are true (T) or false (F).

1 The first speaker wants to spend a week in Canada.
2 The charter flight to Toronto costs £450.
3 The second speaker is extremely worried about possible delays.
4 Her flight leaves Corfu at 03.23 on Saturday 25th.
5 The third speaker has only got hand luggage.
6 He'd prefer a no-smoking seat.
7 The fourth speaker plans to travel alone.
8 She is booking only just in time.

C1

You are going to hear some airport announcements. You are travelling to Pisa and your friend is travelling to Madrid, so listen carefully for information about both of these flights. Answer the questions.

1 Which gate should you go to?
2 What time will your flight depart?
3 Which gate should your friend go to?
4 What time will her flight depart?

C2

Listen again and complete the information.

FLIGHT NUMBER	DESTINATION	DEPARTURE TIME	GATE	ADVICE
BA2724	STOCKHOLM			BOARDING
EAF3310		10.22	32	BOARDING
AF8728	RIGA		11	
KGC934		11.05		BOARDING
	LISBON	11.10		
CA5541		11.25		WAIT IN LOUNGE
	BONN			WAIT IN LOUNGE

D

SPEAKING PRACTICE

Practise these situations with a partner.

1 You are asking for information at a travel agent's, because you're planning next year's holiday.
2 You are booking a flight in person or by phone.
3 You are checking in at the airline desk at the airport, at the start of your holiday.
4 You are confirming flight details for the return trip to your country after your holiday.

Listening tip

Remember that English is spoken by people all round the world, so it's good for you to listen to as many different accents as possible.

10 OUT AND ABOUT

A

Match the words on the left to the words on the right. They all have something to do with entertainment. Use each word once only.

1	film	A	dancer
2	stage	B	singer
3	opera	C	theatre
4	novel	D	reading
5	ballet	E	television
6	quiz show	F	cinema

What are your favourite kinds of entertainment? How often do you go out in the evening? Do you prefer going out alone, with one or two special friends, or with a large group of friends?

B1

You are going to hear a recorded theatre announcement. Look at the words in the box and predict the ones you do NOT expect to hear. Then listen and tick (✔) the words that you hear.

actor	director	musical	reviews
box office	evening	performance	stage
cartoon	film	play	theatre
comedy	matinee	prices	tickets

B2

Listen again and complete the information.

THE GRAND THEATRE, WEXHAM

This week, the Royal Shakespeare (1) _____ in A MIDSUMMER NIGHT'S DREAM by William Shakespeare, from (2) _____ to Saturday. (3) _____ performances at 2.30pm on (4) _____ and Saturday. Evening performances at (5) _____.

Prices from (6) _____ to £22. Next week, for (7) _____ nights only, the (8) _____ London Theatre in A WOMAN IN WHITE, starting at 8pm on (9) _____, Thursday and (10) _____. Prices from £7 to (11) _____.

To book tickets, press (12) _____ on your phone and have your (13) _____ card ready, or ring the (14) _____ office on 01752 (15) _____ .

C1   You are going to hear three young people discussing plans for this evening. Listen and match two of the statements to each speaker.

Harry	A	... accepts the invitation to the cinema.
Adam	B	... dislikes horror films.
Ellie	C	... suggests going to the cinema.
	D	... has seen one film several times.
	E	... enjoys Woody Allen films.
	F	... would prefer a horror film.

C2   Listen again and write down the exact words of the answers to these questions. (Contractions like *he's* count as two words.)

1   Hi Adam, do you fancy seeing a film tonight?

(4 words) _____

2   What do you think, Harry?

(6 words) _____

3   How about it, Ellie?

(5 words) _____

4   Isn't there *any*thing we can agree on?

(9 words) _____

D   **SPEAKING PRACTICE**

Here are some useful ways of accepting or refusing invitations.

Yes, let's. Great idea!   *Yes, why not? What's on?*   *Yes, I'd love to.*
Sorry, I've got something else on.   *I am sorry, I'm afraid I'm busy.*

Practise these situations with a partner.

1   You invite a friend to a rock concert, but s/he has something else planned for that date.
2   You ask someone at work to play squash with you, and s/he likes the idea.
3   You invite your best friend to the cinema tonight, and s/he accepts.
4   You ask someone you don't know well to the theatre. Unfortunately, s/he can't come.

Listening tip   A good way of practising listening is to video English-language films. You can replay them again and again until you understand them really well. Don't worry about words you don't know, just concentrate on the general meaning.

11 HOME SWEET HOME

A

Think about or discuss these questions about homes.

Where would you like to live? In your family home, or in a student hostel?
Would you prefer to live alone, in a flat, or in a room in someone's house? Or you could
share a flat or a house with your friends or other students.
Which would be   a) cheaper?   b) more fun?   c) better for studying?

B1

**You are going to hear a phone conversation between the owner of a flat and someone who
wants to rent a place to live. Read the questions, then listen and answer them.**

1   Who is making the phone call, the man or the woman?
2   What is the woman a bit worried about?
3   Who does most of the talking, the man or the woman, and why?

B2

**Here is Julia's notepad. Listen again
and fill in the information she wants
with *Yes*, *No*, or a different answer.**

Ring Mr Cage about that flat
Address? _____ Edward Road
Self-contained? _____
Large? _____
Warm? _____
Any special advantages?
_____
How much per week? _____
Are bills included? _____
Go and see it tonight? _____
What time? _____

What are the advantages and disadvantages of this flat? Do you think Julia will rent it?
What would *you* do in her situation?

26

C1
You are going to hear Grant and his wife, Sharon, talking about doing some work on their house. Listen and write down the names of the four rooms that they are discussing. They don't name the room that they are in, so you will have to think about this.

C2
Read the sentences, then listen again and match the speakers to the sentences that you hear them say. Use G for Grant and S for Sharon. If Sharon and Grant agree, use B for both.

1 The place still looks a mess. ☐

2 Where do you think we should start? ☐

3 We should throw away that horrible old brown carpet, too. ☐

4 I hate those pink walls! ☐

5 The shower's not working properly. ☐

6 Look how dirty these walls are! ☐

7 It really needs some new wallpaper. ☐

8 We can't do all this ourselves. ☐

D

PRONUNCIATION PRACTICE: /tʃ/ /ʃ/ and /θ/ /ð/ /s/

1 Can you hear the difference between these pairs of words? *Ch* is a much harder sound than *sh*. Listen and repeat the words and sentences after the speaker.

chair, share   watch, wash   cheese, she's   choose, shoes   catch, cash
match, mash   chip, ship   cheap, sheep

Watch out! You'll fall off that chair!
Is she really choosing those shoes?
Shall we share the cash, and watch the match?

2 Here is another group of similar-sounding words. To produce a correct *th* sound, your tongue should be between your teeth. Listen and repeat the words and sentences after the speaker.

thick, sick   worth, worse   think, sink   thumb, some   mouth, mouse
although, also   that, sat

This fog is so thick – it's worse than I thought!
The child put her thumb rather thoughtfully into her mouth.
They sat there, thinking beautiful thoughts about something.

Listening tip
In Grant and Sharon's conversation you can hear some of the 100 most frequently used words in English, for example, *we, to, think, about, a, of, this, do, you, in, and, the, is.* Most conversations are made up of these very short, simple words that you can easily recognise. If you remember this, perhaps it will make you more confident when listening.

12 PHONING AND FOLLOWING
INSTRUCTIONS

A
Match the conversations to the responses in the box.

1 'Is that 887491?'   'No, it's 887492.'
2 'Is Penny there?'   'No, I'm sorry, she's out.'
3 'Mike Barton speaking.'   'Hello, can you switch your fax on, please?'
4 'Hello, can I speak to Simon?'   'Oh, he doesn't live here any more.'
5 'Is Mr Hodge there, please?'   'I'm afraid he's on holiday this week.'

A 'OK, I'll ring back next week then.'	D 'Of course, right away.'
B 'Could you give her a message, please?'	E 'Do you know his new address?'
C 'Oh, sorry, wrong number.'	

B1
You are going to hear three phone conversations. Listen and match the conversations to the descriptions. There is one extra description.

Conversation 1   A a parent asking for help
Conversation 2   B a customer making a complaint
Conversation 3   C a friend giving some news
                      D a driver speaking to a policeman

How do you think the people making the phone calls feel? Choose one adjective from the box for each conversation.

tired   sad   angry   delighted   shocked   worried

B2
Listen again and complete the sentences with ONE word in each gap.

1 The customer has a _____ with the _____ she bought _____.

2 Nothing _____ when she switches it _____.

3 The store will refund her _____, if she takes it back with the _____.

4 Janet has got a new _____.

5 She's going to live in _____.

6 Mrs Jenkins can't _____ where her daughter is.

7 She set out to meet her _____ at _____ o'clock.

8 Her usual _____ for coming home is _____ o'clock.

C1 You are going to hear four people giving instructions on how to use something. Listen and match the speakers 1–4 to the pictures.

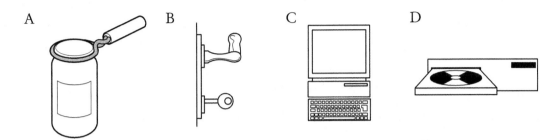

A   B   C   D

C2 Listen again and choose the correct word or phrase you hear from the pair in each box.

Speaker 1   sticky / tricky   idea / ID   the locket / to lock it

push down / pull down

Speaker 2   (properly / probably)   (getting start it / getting started)   (festival / first of all)

(on the keeper / on the keyboard)

Speaker 3   what I do / what I'd do   button here / bottom here   disk in / desk in

Speaker 4   (really well / really will)   (one end of the rubber / one end of the robber)

(holding the hand / holding the handle)

C3 Listen again and choose the right information or opinion from the box for each speaker.

A It's fun to use.   C It's difficult at first.
B It's a good way of solving a problem.   D There's a lot to learn.

D SPEAKING PRACTICE

When you answer the phone in English, you give your name or phone number, or say what your company likes you to say. For example:

Richard speaking.   Richard here.   Richard Smith speaking.
Good morning, Bates and Lunn, Anna speaking. How may I help you?
Essex Arts Club, Steve here. Can I help you?

Here are some more useful expressions to use on the phone:

I'm afraid he's in a meeting.   Could I leave a message?
Just a moment, I'll see if she's in.   Could you ask her to ring me back?
Can I take a message?   Thanks for your help.

Practise phone conversations with a partner.

13 SHOPPING

A

Where can you buy these things? Match each item to the right kind of shop. (You can buy some things at several different shops.)

baker's

post office

chemist's

newsagent's

butcher's

greengrocer's

department store

supermarket

boutique

Do you prefer buying food in small shops or at supermarkets? How often do you go shopping for food or clothes?

B1

You are going to hear a conversation between Zoë and George, who are planning to have a picnic with some friends. Listen and tick (✔) all the items that they are going to buy.

beef	fruit juice	peaches
bread	lemonade	potatoes
butter	lettuce	radishes
carrots	mayonnaise	salad dressing
cheese	milk	strawberries
chicken	oil	tomatoes
crisps	olives	tuna
cucumber	onions	white wine
eggs	pasta	

B2

Listen again and complete the sentences from the conversation.

1 OK, that's great! Now _____ list?

2 Oh yes! _____ a tin of tuna?

3 What _____ need? Oh yes, the drinks.

4 And lots and lots of strawberries – _____!

What do you think of George and Zoë's plans for the picnic?

C1 Listen to the man's story and answer the questions by ticking the correct answer.

1 What was the first present the man bought for his girlfriend?

A 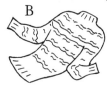 B  C  D

2 Where did he buy it?

A  B  C

3 What did he change it for?

A  B 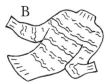 C  D

4 Where did the second girl in the story live?
   A in the next house
   B in the flat above the man
   C in the house opposite
   D in the next street

C2 Listen again and tick (✔) the correct sentences.

1 He went to more than one shop to choose the present.
2 He knew his girlfriend disliked red.
3 He wasn't sure of his girlfriend's size.
4 He gave the blouse to the girl next door because she liked it.
5 His girlfriend didn't mind seeing the girl next door wearing the green blouse.

D SPEAKING PRACTICE

Here are some useful expressions to use when shopping for clothes.

SHOP ASSISTANT: *Good morning, can I help you?*
   CUSTOMER: *Yes, have you got any swimsuits in stock?* *How much is this jacket?*
   I'd like a scarf/a pair of socks/some tights, please.
   Can I try on this suit, please? *Are there any other colours?*
   I think I need a bigger/smaller size.
   Have you got this in a size 38, please?
   Yes, I'll take it. Can I pay by credit card?

Practise conversations with a partner; one person is the customer, the other is the shop assistant.

14 IT'S A SMALL WORLD

Think about or discuss these questions.

Have you ever met someone you know in a strange place, completely unexpectedly?
Why do people say 'It's a small world?' Do you agree or not?

Have you ever visited the United States? If so, which places did you visit? If not, where would you like to go?

B1

You are going to hear a woman telling a story about her trip to the USA. Look at the map, then listen and mark the route that she took.

B2

Read the questions, then listen again and answer them.

1   How long ago did the woman's story happen?
2   Why did she go to the USA?
3   How long did she stay in New York?
4   How did she travel around the country?
5   What part of her trip did she enjoy most?
6   Where did she meet her brother?
7   Why was it a surprise?
8   Why was it lucky for him?

C1

You are going to hear another traveller talking about a recent holiday that he had with his wife in India. Read the statements, then listen and tick (✔) the correct ones.

1 It was an expensive holiday.
2 They want to get all their money back.
3 The holiday lasted for two weeks.
4 They stayed in a 5-star hotel.
5 They were expecting to get three meals a day.
6 There were some good points about the holiday.

C2

Listen again and complete the notes the man made during his holiday.

<u>Holiday in India</u>

With _____ company
Hotel name: **the Shelton (Hyderabad)**
Number of days: _____
Total cost: _____
<u>Problems</u>
Room: a)_____ b)_____
Food: a)_____ b)_____
Service: _____
Waiters: _____
Excursions: a)_____ b)_____
Action to take: **Get some of our money back!**

D

PRONUNCIATION PRACTICE: Short and long vowels

Listen and repeat these words after the speaker.

sit, seat	dip, deep	hill, heal	chip, cheap	hit, heat	fill, feel	wick, weak
got, goat	rod, road	Tod, toad	doll, dole	mop, mope	hop, hope	
fat, fate	hat, hate	mac, make	back, bake	sack, sake	rack, rake	
lit, light	bit, bite	mitt, might	hit, height	Brit, bright	sit, sight	

15 MEETING AND GREETING

A

What words do you use when you meet people or when you say goodbye? Match each picture to one of the speech bubbles. There is one extra speech bubble.

A   B   C   D

1 So sorry I'm late – I got stuck in a traffic jam!

2 I'll give you a ring very soon – OK?

3 No, no, it's my turn to pay!

4 Come and stay with us any time – my parents would love to see you.

5 Jack, do you know Nathan Oliver? Jack Bennett, Nathan Oliver.

B1

You are going to hear four short conversations. Read the statements, then listen and decide whether they are true (T) or false (F).

1 Joshua and Megan haven't seen each other for years.
2 Joshua now lives in Seattle.
3 Nathan Oliver has worked for the company longer than Jack Bennett.
4 Jack Bennett has an interesting idea for Nathan Oliver.
5 Emma was travelling by bus to meet her friend.
6 Rebecca got wet because she had to walk there.
7 Emma and Rebecca were planning to go to the theatre.
8 The two men have just had a meal.
9 They are brothers.

B2

Listen again and decide how the people sound. Choose TWO adjectives each time.

1 The woman: interested   busy   sociable
   The man: forgetful   in a hurry   friendly

2 The woman: in control   positive   tired
   The new assistant: business-like   polite   unsure

3 First girl: surprised   cross   sorry
   Second girl: sad   angry   critical

4 The two men: relaxed   generous   hungry

C1

You are going to hear two people meeting at a party. Listen and tick (✔) the words that you hear.

chocolate	hobbies	jobs	life	smell
company	home	lab	news	taste
friend	jackets	leather	scientist	work

C2

Listen again and choose from A, B or C to complete the sentences correctly.

1 Charlie and Rachel   A   are friends.
  B   work in the same office.
  C   have just met for the first time.

2 Charlie works   A   for Gucci.
  B   with Annette.
  C   for Prada.

3 Charlie   A   buys jackets.
  B   buys leather.
  C   wears leather jackets.

4 Rachel works   A   in a lab.
  B   in a kitchen.
  C   at a chemist's.

5 Rachel   A   makes chocolate.
  B   enjoys eating chocolate.
  C   tastes chocolate.

D

PRONUNCIATION PRACTICE: Chunking

When you listen to English, you hear people pausing between groups of words or sounds (sometimes called 'chunks'). A pause often shows that there's going to be a change in meaning, or a new idea, or some extra information. Listen to these sentences from Exercise C, and mark where you hear a pause.

1 Yes I used to work with her actually at Prada.
2 Oh really what do you do?
3 Well actually I used to love chocolate.
4 Let me get you another drink tomato juice was it?

Listen and repeat the sentences after the speaker, pausing in the correct places.

Listening tip

If you are listening to a tape, concentrate on the most important facts the first time you listen. Think about the background, and imagine yourself in that situation. Then, when you listen for the second or third time, you will be able to catch the details.

16 THE QUEEN'S HOUSE

A

Think about or discuss these questions about visiting old buildings.

What kind of information would you want to find out if you visited an old house where people lived hundreds of years ago?
What words would you expect to hear from a tour guide in an old house or palace?

B1

Look at the floor plan of the Queen's House in Greenwich, and the list of rooms. Listen to the guided tour of the house and fill in the names of the rooms on the plan.

King's Stateroom	Queen's Stateroom
King's Waiting Room	Queen's Waiting Room
King's Bedroom	Queen's Bedroom
Music Room	Dining Room
Library	Study
King's Bathroom	Maid's Room

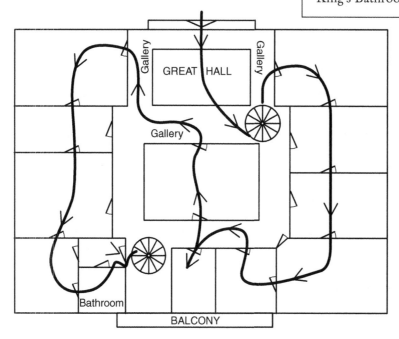

B2

Listen again and answer the questions. Choose the correct answer (A, B or C).

1 Where is the Queen's House?
  A in Denmark   B in Italy   C in London

2 Who did the house first belong to?
  A Inigo Jones   B Anne of Denmark   C Charles I

3 The house was built between
  A 1616 and 1635.   B 1635 and 1716.   C 1660 and 1735.

4 The black and white marble floor is in
  A the Gallery.   B the Great Hall.   C the King's Bathroom.

5 Which is the 'most richly-furnished' room in the house?
   A the King's Stateroom   B the Great Hall   C the King's Waiting-room
6 Which room is just like the King's Bedroom?
   A the King's Stateroom   B the Bathroom   C the Queen's Bedroom

C1 You are going to hear a conversation between a couple who have just visited the Queen's House. Listen and tick (✔) the words that you hear.

boat trip	cheap	cost	restaurant	tea
bus	chips	market	shopping	visit
café	coach trip	museum	taxi	visitor

C2 Listen again and complete the sentences from the conversation.

1 Now, what shall we _____ next?

2 I'm not going anywhere. My _____.

3 How about _____ on the River Thames?

4 You spend _____ at home.

5 How much _____?

6 They do a lovely _____ in the National Gallery restaurant.

7 But I warn you, next year _____ home.

8 You can _____ on your own!

D PRONUNCIATION PRACTICE: / h / and -ough

1 Listen and repeat these words after the speaker, making sure you pronounce the h sound.

hello   hair   Harry   his   hers   happy   hurry   horse   haunted   house

Harry's on holiday in Honolulu in a haunted house.
Have you heard, horse-riding makes Helen happy?

2 -ough is a difficult sound in English, because there are several different ways of pronouncing it. Listen and repeat after the speaker.

rough, tough, enough
thorough, borough
thought, bought, sought, fought
cough   through

I thought I'd bought a tough pair of shoes.
She coughed all through the night.
It's a rough borough to live in.

17 FREE TIME

A   What are your spare-time interests and how much time do you spend on them? Match the pictures to five of these activities.

rock climbing	reading	going to the cinema
parachuting	driving fast cars	birdwatching
sailing	travelling	

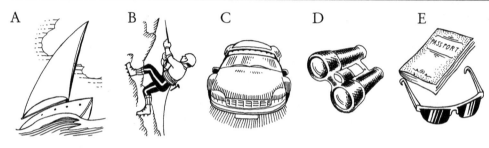

A   B   C   D   E

B1   You are going to hear a recorded message, giving information about summer study courses in a country house. Listen and number the courses in the order that you hear them mentioned.

Family History	Intensive Russian	Writing Short Stories
Intensive French	Modern Art	Yoga
Intensive Japanese	Tennis	
Intensive Portuguese	Understanding the Internet	

B2   Read the statements, then listen again and decide whether they are true (T) or false (F).

At Little Stoke Manor this summer ...

1   ... the new programme starts next week.
2   ... you can study Portuguese and French at the same time.
3   ... David Malcolm will teach for two weeks.
4   ... you can practise tennis in a group.
5   ... Lizzie Windrush will talk about family history.
6   ... yoga is a new course.
7   ... yoga is available only at weekends.
8   ... Peter Dennis is the computer expert.
9   ... you can study Modern Art in June.
10   ... you should ring 0191 48765 to book.

C1 You are going to hear two friends, Scott and Melissa, discussing fitness centres in their area. Listen and complete the information in the table.

Name	What's available	Price	Where	Phone number
1 Sweatshop	_____ weights	_____	Town centre	_____
2 _____	gym, _____ yoga	£180 a year	Near station	_____
3 _____	_____, sauna _____, aerobics free car park	_____	Out of town	

C2 Listen again and choose the exact words (A, B, C or D) used by the speakers.

1 A That's a good price, isn't it?
   B That's cheap, isn't it?
   C That's very reasonable.
   D This isn't very expensive.

2 A What's on offer there?
   B What facilities has it got?
   C What's available there?
   D What equipment has it got?

3 A You could travel by train.
   B You could take the train.
   C You could come in on the train.
   D You could arrive by train.

4 A Maybe this one's worth a look.
   B This one may be OK.
   C Maybe this one is suitable.
   D This one may be what we want.

D SPEAKING PRACTICE

People often ask and answer questions about their hobbies like this.

A: *What do you do in your spare time?*   B: *Well, I like computer games and ...*
A: *Do you belong to any clubs?*   B: *Yes, I'm a member of my local swimming club.*
A: *How long have you been interested in old clocks?*   B: *For about the last three years.*
A: *How often do you watch football?*   B: *Whenever I have time, about once a week.*

With a partner, practise conversations like these about your own hobbies.

Listening tip   Use your hobbies and spare-time activities to practise your listening. If you like pop music, for example, try writing down the words of any of your favourite songs. If you like the cinema, watch out for films in English. If you like listening to the radio or watching TV, tune into English-language channels, like the BBC or CNN.

18 DANGER!

A

Match the words in the box to their meanings. You are going to hear them in Part B, so you need to know what they mean.

1 when a boat turns over in the water
2 a large sailing boat
3 the floor of a boat
4 when there are a lot of waves
5 a large ship for people, cars and lorries, taking the same route regularly
6 a kind of waistcoat with air in it, that you should wear when sailing, to keep you up if you fall into the water

life-jacket	yacht
deck	capsize
ferry	rough sea

B1

Listen to Sam's story and put the pictures in the right order.

B2

Listen again and decide whether the sentences are true (T) or false (F).

1 Sam has never had a more dangerous experience.
2 Alice knows his yacht.
3 This all happened last summer.
4 He was sailing from North Wales to Northern Ireland.
5 There were four men on the boat.
6 Only two of them were wearing life-jackets.
7 They all sat on top of the capsized boat.
8 The ferry changed its route in order to pick them up.

Mark on the map where you think the accident happened.

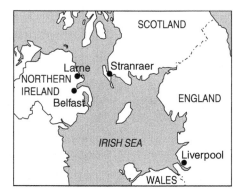

C1 You are going to hear two people talking about a trip to New Zealand. Look at the pictures, then listen and tick (✔) the things that they mention.

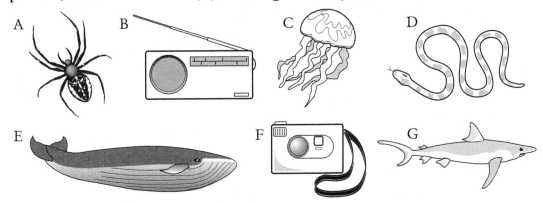

A   B   C   D

E   F   G

C2 Read the 'Possible danger' column, then listen again and complete the 'Action to take' column.

Possible danger	Action to take
1 You meet a shark when diving in the sea.	The best thing to do is …
2 You see a jellyfish close to you when you're swimming.	It's a good thing to …
3 A small black spider with a red patch bites you.	You'll have to …
4 You're travelling with all your luggage in your car. You want to park and walk along the beach.	You shouldn't …

D **PRONUNCIATION PRACTICE:**   Falling intonation and sentence stress

Most sentences in English end with a falling tone, when your voice goes *down* at the end. Listen and repeat after the speaker.

1 I'd never been there.
2 It's later than I thought.
3 They've planted two apple trees.
4 The flight takes five hours.
5 We'll have to pay the bills this week.
6 She's bought a cottage in the country.
7 You'll always be welcome.
8 She's a very good writer.
9 What a lovely day!
10 He often arrives late.

Now underline the words where you think there is a strong stress. Listen again and repeat after the speaker, making sure that you use correct stress *and* bring your voice down at the end of each sentence.

19 TOWN AND COUNTRY

A

What are the advantages or disadvantages of living in the town, or in the country?
Where would *you* prefer to live?

B1

You are going to hear a conversation between two women, Amy and Jessica. Read the
questions and look at the pictures, then listen and answer the questions by ticking (✔)
the right pictures.

1 What kind of job does Amy do?

2 Where does Jessica work?

3 Why does Amy think roads are sometimes dangerous in the country?

B2

Read the questions, then listen again and answer them.

1 Does Jessica know Amy well or not? How do you know?
2 What exactly is Amy's job?
3 Why do farmers need her?
4 How does Jessica feel about Amy's job?
5 What nearly happened to Amy this morning?
6 What does Amy like about working in the country?

C1 Listen to this conversation between Rory and Patsy and decide whether the statements are true (T) or false (F).

1 Rory and Patsy went to the theatre together.
2 The theatre opened recently.
3 Rory saw the play at the Edinburgh Festival.
4 The last bus to Winterbourne leaves at 11 p.m.
5 Rory enjoyed the busy atmosphere on the streets.
6 He went to Café Prague by taxi.
7 He thinks the evening was too expensive.

C2 Listen again and complete Patsy's questions or comments.

1 Hi Rory! Did you _____?

2 Oh. Where _____?

3 How long's _____?

4 Oh brilliant! Did you go _____?

5 I bet that _____.

6 You should _____!

D **PRONUNCIATION PRACTICE: Rising and falling intonation**

English speakers usually make their voices go up at the end of a sentence if they are asking a question and expecting a *Yes/No* answer. Listen and repeat these questions after the speaker, with a rising intonation.

1 Are you sure it's number 2?
2 Did you lock the door?
3 Is there a shop that sells milk?
4 Do *you* always walk the dog?
5 Do you live near the school?
6 Has he lived there for long?
7 Are you on holiday next week?
8 Is it the first today?
9 Did they come by bus?
10 Have you seen the doctor yet?

Now look at these questions and decide whether your voice should rise (if it's a *Yes/No* question) or fall (if it asks for information). Mark them UP or DOWN at the end of the sentence. Listen and check.

11 How are you today?
12 Can you swim?
13 What's your name?
14 Have you got a bike?
15 Where does she live?
16 Why are you late?
17 Have you got any pets?
18 Do you speak Arabic?
19 How much did that cost?
20 Do you like him?

Listen again and repeat numbers 11–20 after the speaker.

20 SCHOOL AND COLLEGE

A

Think about or discuss these questions about education.

What age do children start school and leave school in your country?
Which do you think is better, a state school or a private school, and why?
Is it a good idea to study at college/university?
Do you think university students work hard or not?

B1

You are going to hear five people talking about school, or about their work or studies. Listen and tick (✔) the words that you hear.

break	freedom	lunches	science	teacher
children	games	money	stories	timetable
exams	lessons	pupils	studying	uniforms

B2

Listen again and match the speakers to the correct information. There are two extra pieces of information.

Speaker 1   A ... is still a school pupil.
Speaker 2   B ... no longer works as a teacher.
Speaker 3   C ... works as a school cleaner.
Speaker 4   D ... teaches part-time.
Speaker 5   E ... really liked his/her school.
              F ... is a university student.
              G ... has children who are at school.

C1 You are going to hear two students, Liam and Jade, discussing university life. Read the statements about them, then listen and tick (✔) the correct ones.

Liam 1 ... is studying science.
        2 ... works in the lab for eight hours a day.
        3 ... thinks he works harder than Jade.
Jade 4 ... is planning to miss her next lecture.
        5 ... doesn't have to go to all her lectures.
        6 ... spends every weekend studying.

C2 Listen again and choose the exact words (A, B or C) used by the speakers.

1 A I've just got time before my next lecture.
    B There's just time before the lecture.
    C I'm just in time for the lesson.
2 A There are two men with us for that.
    B It's too much money for us.
    C There are too many of us for that.
3 A It's so relaxing doing arts.
    B Things are so relaxed for you arts people.
    C This is so relaxing for you and Art.
4 A Things are twice as hard for you.
    B My work's twice as hard as yours.
    C I think I work twice as hard as you do.
5 A What happened last week then?
    B How about last weekend then?
    C What about last weekend then?

D PRONUNCIATION PRACTICE: Word stress

It is very important to stress parts of words correctly because if you don't, people may not understand you. Listen and repeat after the speaker.

1 interesting   telephone   awfully   letter   secretary   sandwich   finish   project
2 potato   tomato   ridiculous   amusing   employer   banana   graffiti   reporter
3 weekend   hotel   shampoo   engineer   mayonnaise   kangaroo   referee

Where does the stress come in each of the three groups of words?

Now listen and repeat these sentences after the speaker.

The secretary received an awfully interesting letter from her employer.
The engineer spent a quiet weekend in a hotel, before finishing his project.
Would you like mayonnaise in your tomato sandwich?

21 WHAT'S THE PROBLEM?

A

Find pairs of opposite adjectives, used for describing people.

modest	talkative	cruel	quiet	energetic
nervous	tired	proud	relaxed	kind

Which words would you like people to use when describing you? Can you use these words to describe any famous people you know?

B1

A girl and a boy, Bella and Lewis, have a problem with their relationship. You are going to hear part of a radio phone-in programme, which tries to help people with their problems. First you are going to hear Bella giving *her* side of the story. Read the questions first, then listen and answer them.

1 How long have they been going out together?
2 What type of person is Lewis?
3 What was Bella trying to tell him about?
4 Why is she worried about Lewis?
5 Can you guess why Lewis is behaving like this?

B2

Now you are going to hear Lewis's side of the story. Read the questions first, then listen and answer them.

1 What is Lewis's job?
2 How does he feel in the evenings, and why?
3 How does Bella feel in the evenings, and why?
4 Why doesn't Lewis talk much? Complete the sentences.

   a) He doesn't find it easy to _____.

   b) Bella _____ too much.
5 When does he 'switch off', and why?
6 Who doesn't like Bella much, and why?

Can you help to solve their problem? Decide what advice to give Bella or Lewis and write a letter to one of them.

C1

Luke has a Russian penfriend, Alexei. Instead of writing a letter to Alexei, Luke has recorded what he wants to say on cassette. Listen and match the names to the pictures. There is one extra picture.

| Auntie Joan | Dad | Josie | Granny | Mum |

What is Luke's problem? Is it a real problem?

C2

Listen again and decide whether the statements are true (T) or false (F).

1 Alexei has already written to Luke.
2 Luke's father works in a restaurant kitchen.
3 Luke's mother broke her leg playing tennis.
4 Josie and Luke have different opinions about homework.
5 Luke's Granny started knitting at the age of 80.
6 Auntie Joan lives with Luke's family.
7 Auntie Joan and Spot don't have any breakfast.
8 Luke wants his family to change.

D

SPEAKING PRACTICE

Here are some ways of making suggestions.

Why don't we talk about it?   *What about spending more time together?*
Shall we ask someone's advice?   *How about telling her how you feel?*
Let's discuss it now.   *Why don't you ask what the problem is?*

And here are some possible answers.

Great idea!   *Yes, why not?*   *OK, I'll do that.*   *Yes, I think we should.*

Think of your own suggestions. Practise them, and the answers, with a partner.

22 MONEY MATTERS

What words or phrases are you likely to hear or use when talking about money?
Tick (✔) the words in the box that have something to do with money.

account	coin	income	recipe	traveller's cheques
bench	credit card	lend	savings	wallpaper
bill	currently	menu	sheep	
burger	debit card	pocket money	steel	
cash	expensive	pounds	tip	

B1

You are going to hear a man telling a story. Look at the pictures first, then listen and put them in the right order.

A   B   C   D

B2

Listen again and choose from A, B, C or D to complete the sentences correctly.

1 The man and his wife were   A in Italy on business.
                                 B on holiday on the French Riviera.
                                 C on holiday in Italy.

2 They were staying   A in a hotel.
                       B with friends.
                       C in rooms over a restaurant.

3 The man always pays by credit card   A at lunch-time.
                                          B if a meal costs a lot.
                                          C if he's with his wife.

4 He didn't have his card because   A he had lost it.
                                       B someone stole it.
                                     C it was in his other trousers.

5 He didn't tell his wife he didn't have the card, because
   A she didn't have enough money to pay.
   B it would spoil her birthday.
   C she might be angry with him.

6 The meal plus tip cost
   A more than 180,000 lire.
   B less than 180,000 lire.
   C 180,000 lire exactly.

C1

You are going to hear a phone call to a bank. Read the questions, then listen and answer them.

1 Which bank is it?
2 What is the speaker phoning about?

3 What is the speaker's name?
4 What will the bank do now?

C2

These sentences from the phone call are in the wrong order. Listen again and put them in the correct order.

A   You want some details, yes, right, I'm Victoria P. Brane, got that?
B   And the card number's 4989 1662 3972 1408.
C   Hello, is that the Midland Bank, the emergency help line?
D   So can you cancel it or something, you know, whatever?
E   At least I *think* I've lost it, but maybe it was stolen.
F   So is that it – you're going to cancel my card and send me a new one?
G   Victoria like the queen or the station, OK?
H   Oh good – look, this really *is* an emergency.
I   Anyway, I haven't got it any more.
J   Then P for, well, I won't tell you what it's for, it's such a silly name, and then Brane, that's B.R.A.N.E.
K   The thing is, I've lost my card, my debit card, you know.
L   Then I won't have to pay if somebody else uses it, that's how it works, isn't it?

D

SPEAKING PRACTICE

Here is an 'alphabet shopping' game to help improve your vocabulary – and memory!

The first person starts by saying, '*I went into town yesterday and bought an APPLE*' (or other word beginning with A). The second person says, '*I went into town yesterday and bought an APPLE and a BOOK*' (or other word beginning with B). The next person says, '*I went into town and bought an APPLE, a BOOK and a COMPUTER.*' The game continues round the class, using all the letters from A to Z. You can play this game on your own, too.

> *Listening tip*
>
> Listen for the rising and falling tunes of English conversation. If the voice falls at the end of a sentence, it means the speaker has finished talking, but if the voice goes up at the end of a sentence, you know that the speaker is expecting an answer from you, or perhaps hasn't finished speaking yet.

23 FINDING YOUR WAY

A

Match the questions to the answers.

1 Could you tell me where I can find a taxi?
2 Could you tell me the way to the bus station?
3 Is it far?
4 What number bus should I take for the museum?

A Yes, turn left and it's at the bottom of the hill.
B I think it's the 27A, or the 5B.
C There are some waiting in North Street.
D No, only five minutes' walk.

B1

You are going to hear someone giving directions. Listen and number the places in the box in the order that you hear them.

bank	crossroads	roundabout
church	Dyke Road	Royal Alexandra Hospital
Clifton Road	MacBurgers	station
Clock Tower	roadworks	traffic lights

B2

Listen again and fill in Clifton Road and Dyke Road on the map, and mark the suggested route.

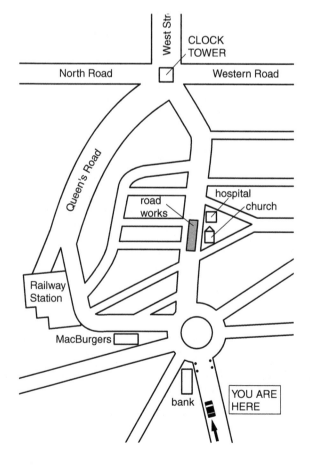

50

C1 You are going to hear two people talking about losing their way. Listen to the man and answer questions 1–3. Then listen to the woman and answer questions 4–6.

1 Where were the man and his friend?
2 How were they travelling?
3 How many times did they see the same policeman?
4 How was the woman travelling?
5 What was she looking for?
6 Did she take the driver's advice?

Which story does the picture show?

C2 Listen to the two people again and complete the sentences.

1 It was hard to find the hotel, because _____.

2 When the policeman saw them for the second time, _____.

3 In the end, one of the policemen _____.

4 The woman didn't know the way to the hostel, so _____.

5 The driver advised her not _____.

6 Unfortunately, she _____, so she got lost.

7 The driver and the policeman both _____.

8 The man and the woman were both helped _____.

D SPEAKING PRACTICE

With a partner, practise asking the way and giving directions to these places.

1 the nearest post office in your town
2 the tourist office
3 the main railway station
4 the hospital
5 the nearest bank/bookshop/newsagent's

Listening tip Remember that many English words have the same sound, but a different spelling and a different meaning, for example:

tail, tale   see, sea   flower, flour   heard, herd   road, rode   break, brake
been, bean   made, maid   father, farther   leak, leek   piece, peace

Just concentrate on what the words mean in the sentence that you are listening to.

24 PEOPLE

A Find pairs of opposite adjectives, used for describing people.

shy	sad	kind	mean	cruel	quiet
polite	happy	unsure	noisy	unselfish	
rude	sociable	generous	confident	selfish	

What kind of person are you? Describe yourself, using some of the adjectives in the box.

B1 You are going to hear descriptions of five people. Look at the pictures, then listen and number the objects in the order that you hear them.

A $3X + 8 = 17$

B2 Read the statements, then listen again and choose the correct statement for each person. There are two extra statements.

1 Claudia
2 Jim
3 Miss Henderson
4 Gary
5 Mr Lewis

A ... earns a good salary as a musician.
B ... often goes shopping.
C ... wants to look fashionable.
D ... likes animals.
E ... believes in luck.
F ... doesn't worry about money.
G ... was good at the job.

C1

You are going to hear some more information about the five people. Listen and complete the paragraphs, using ONE word for each gap.

1 Claudia comes from Dunbar, (1) _____ Edinburgh. She is (2) _____ years old. She comes from a (3) _____ family. She finds it very (4) _____ to meet people, and doesn't like (5) _____ out.

2 Jim's parents are both (1)_____. The whole family are very (2) _____, and they play in (3) _____ together. He always says (4) _____ to you when he sees you, and even holds (5) _____ open.

3 Miss Henderson had a (1) _____ once, a long time (2) _____. But she never got (3) _____ because she had to look after her elderly (4) _____. So she gave up her freedom and her (5) _____ of getting married.

4 Gary spends a lot of money on (1) _____. Luckily, he has a good (2) _____, with a high salary – he works in his father's company. He spends money on his friends, too, especially on their (3) _____.

5 Everyone at the local school (1) _____ Mr Lewis. He was a (2) _____ teacher. Now he's retired, he doesn't seem to have any (3) _____, and he spends a lot of time on his (4) _____. I don't think he looks very (5) _____.

C2

Listen again and choose the adjective from Exercise A which best describes each person.

1 Claudia _____   4 Gary _____

2 Jim _____   5 Mr Lewis _____

3 Miss Henderson _____

D

SPEAKING PRACTICE

Find out about people you are interested in. Ask these questions.

What's his/her name?   *How old is he/she?*
Where does he/she live?   *What does he/she do?*
What is he/she interested in?   *What kind of person is he/she?*

Ask a partner about (a) his/her brother or sister (b) his/her parents (c) his/her best friend (d) his/her teacher.

Listening tip

Talking to English-speaking people is a good way of practising your listening. Even if they talk fast, try to understand, and ask questions if necessary. Taking part in real conversations will make you more confident when listening.

25 HAPPY FAMILIES

A **Think about or discuss these questions about your family.**

What is your family like? How many brothers and sisters have you got? Are they older or younger than you? Do your grandparents, or your aunts, uncles and cousins live with you?

B1 **Look at the pictures, then listen to four people talking about their families. Match the speakers 1–4 to the pictures.**

B2 **Listen again and decide which sentence (A, B or C) best describes the way the people feel about their families.**

Speaker 1   A He liked living in a quiet house.
            B He didn't enjoy being an only child.
            C He remembers his parents laughing a lot.

Speaker 2   A She likes living with her cousins.
            B She wishes her sisters could live with them.
            C She thinks their house is too big.

Speaker 3   A Living away from home makes him unhappy.
            B It's not easy living with an old lady.
            C He enjoys his grandmother's cooking.

Speaker 4   A She wants to help her mother.
            B She often tells her brothers what to do.
            C Things have changed now that there's a new dog in the house.

How do you get on with your family? Do you ever argue with your brothers and sisters or your parents? If so, what do you argue about? And who usually wins the argument?

C1 You are going to hear a woman talking about her family. Look at the family tree, then listen and fill in the gaps with the names in the box.

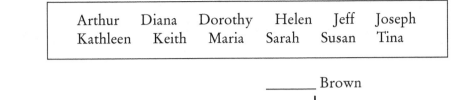

Arthur	Diana	Dorothy	Helen	Jeff	Joseph
Kathleen	Keith	Maria	Sarah	Susan	Tina

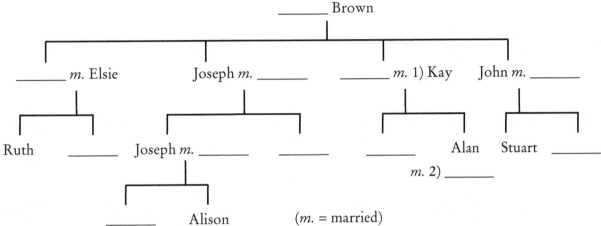

_____ Brown

_____ *m.* Elsie Joseph *m.* _____ _____ *m.* 1) Kay John *m.* _____

Ruth _____ Joseph *m.* _____ _____ _____ Alan Stuart _____

m. 2) _____

_____ Alison (*m.* = married)

C2 Listen again and answer the questions.

1 What relation is Helen to Keith?
2 What relation is Jeff to the speaker?
3 What is the speaker's name?
4 What relation are Sarah and Alison to the speaker?
5 How many people in the family share the same name, and what is it?

D PRONUNCIATION PRACTICE: Verb endings

Listen to the ten sentences and choose the verb you hear from the pair in each box. Watch out for the different endings of English verb forms.

1 play / played	2 watch / watches	3 run / runs	4 cook / cooked

5 take / takes	6 pass / passed	7 wash / washed

8 write / writes	9 walks / walked	10 looks / looked

Listen again and repeat the sentences after the speaker, making sure you pronounce the verb endings correctly.

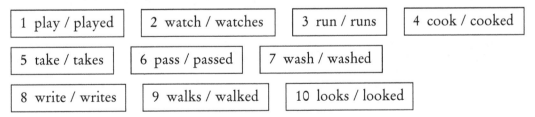

Listening tip

When you are listening to English, keep eye contact with the speaker. Use your face to show you are interested. You can also help the speaker along by nodding your head from time to time, or by saying encouraging things like 'Really?', 'Well!', 'Did you?'

26 THE WORLD OF WORK

A **Match the pictures to eight of the jobs in the box.**

A

B

C

D

E

F

G

H

baker	gardener	teacher
doctor	greengrocer	vet
farmer	lifeguard	waitress
firefighter	secretary	window-cleaner

Would you like to do any of these jobs? What jobs do people in your family do?
Choose two of the jobs and compare them. What are their advantages and disadvantages?

B1 **You are going to hear four speakers talking about their work. Look at the jobs in the box above, then listen and tick (✔) the ones that you hear.**

B2 **Listen again and match the speakers to the reasons they give for changing their jobs. There are three extra reasons.**

Speaker 1	A ... wanted more free time.
Speaker 2	B ... did not like the boss.
Speaker 3	C ... wanted to earn more money.
Speaker 4	D ... moved to another town.
	E ... wanted to work with animals.
	F ... got married.
	G ... had an accident.

What do you think are the best reasons for changing jobs?

C1 You are going to hear a man talking about his life and career. Read the questions, then listen and answer them.

1 Which languages can he speak?
2 What nationality was his mother?
3 Did he enjoy teaching?
4 Why did he become a writer?

C2 These sentences describe his life so far, but they are in the wrong order. Listen again and put them in the right order.

A He moved to Paris.
B He taught foreign languages to private pupils.
C He bought a large house overlooking the sea.
D He won a prize for his writing.
E He was born in a city in the United Kingdom.
F His best pupil was a count.
G He studied at Munich University.
H He became a writer of detective stories.
I He moved to Austria.

D PRONUNCIATION PRACTICE: Similar sounds

Listen to some phrases from the recording and choose the correct word or phrase you hear from each pair in the box.

1 grown up / growing up	7 German / Germany
2 Chichester / Manchester	8 in a palace / Indianapolis
3 Harris / Paris	9 writer / lighter
4 France / French	10 1919 / 1990
5 Austria / Australia	11 Turkey / Torquay
6 teacher / preacher	12 walked home / worked at home

Listen and repeat these words or phrases after the speaker, making sure your pronunciation is very clear.

Listening tip Don't just listen to the words, listen for clues in the tone of voice. Is the speaker angry, or bored, or sad? Look at people's body language, which could help you to understand what they really mean. For example, someone receiving flowers might say, *'Oh, you shouldn't have!'* If you just listen to the words, you might think that giving the flowers was wrong or a mistake, but if you look at their body language, you will realise how pleased they are.

27 WHAT LOVELY WEATHER!

A Match the symbols to the kind of weather that they represent. You are going to use them in Exercise B1.

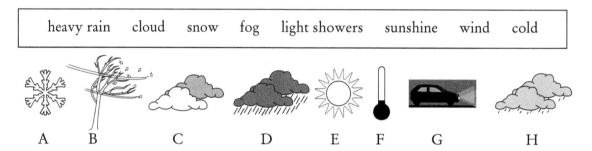

| heavy rain | cloud | snow | fog | light showers | sunshine | wind | cold |

A   B   C   D   E   F   G   H

B1 Look at the map of Scotland, then listen to the weather forecast. Write one of the letters (A–H) from above beside each place on the map, to show what kind of weather it is going to get.

B2 Listen again and answer the questions.

1 Which place will have the most sunshine tomorrow?
2 What will the top temperature be there?
3 Why must you be careful if you're driving in Edinburgh?
4 Is it unusual for the outer Hebrides to be rainy?
5 What will the maximum temperature be in Glasgow tomorrow?
6 What kind of weather will the Orkney Islands get soon (not tomorrow)?
7 What kind of weather can the Scots expect for next week?

C1 You are going to hear two neighbours talking about a recent holiday. Read the questions, then listen and answer them.

1 Where did Grace go on holiday?
2 What was the weather problem she experienced?
3 Did she stay in the same hotel for the whole holiday?
4 Which weather conditions does she complain of?
5 What was the weather like at home while she was away?

C2 Listen to these phrases from the recording and choose the correct phrase you hear from each pair in the box.

1 for the four weeks / for the first week	7 poor you / for you
2 hear about it / hereabouts	8 we want it to / we wanted to do
3 awful tornado / or full tornado	9 it's a real leaf / it's a relief
4 to another hotel / to the other hotel	10 I can tell you / I can't tell you
5 nobody was heard / nobody was hurt	11 on the home / on the whole
6 really quite cold / really quiet cold	12 just very cold / usefully cold

D SPEAKING PRACTICE

This is the sort of thing people often say when talking about the weather.

A: *What a lovely day!*   B: *Yes, it is, isn't it?*
A: *It rained terribly hard yesterday, didn't it?*   B: *Yes, it did, didn't it?*
A: *It's never been as cold as this in June before!*   B: *No, it hasn't, has it?*

The politeness rule is that, in a conversation about the weather, you almost always agree with the other person.

What should you say if someone talks to you about the weather? Match the sentences to the replies and then practise short conversations about the weather with a partner.

1 *We had a much better summer in 1976!*   A *Yes, it did, didn't it?*
2 *It did snow heavily yesterday.*   B *No, it hasn't, has it?*
3 *I think it's going to rain.*   C *Yes, we did, didn't we?*
4 *It was cloudier this morning.*   D *Yes, it is, isn't it?*
5 *It's never rained so much in April before!* E *Yes, it was, wasn't it?*

Listening tip Just before a listening test, make sure you talk to your friends in English, or if you can't do that, think in English. Ask and answer questions in your head, for example:
How long is this test going to last?
How many people are there in the room?
What kind of vocabulary will there be in the test?
This will make it easier for you to 'tune in' to listening in English.

28 GAME, SET AND MATCH!

A   **Match the pictures to eight of these sporting activities.**

basketball	rugby	baseball	riding	darts
hockey	tennis	skiing	golf	snooker

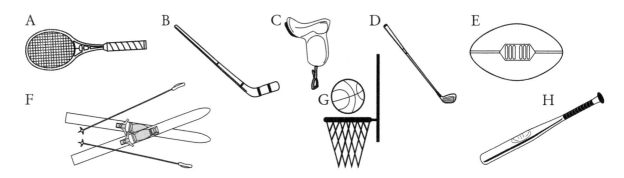

What is your favourite sport? Which is the most popular sport in your country?
Do you prefer watching or playing?

B1   **You are going to hear four sports people talking about their lives. Listen and tick (✔) the words that you hear.**

champion	football	manager	practice	team
cup	income	match	prize	training
exercise	lifestyle	money	sport	trips

B2   **Listen again and fill in the table.**

Name	Sport	What he/she is doing now	Future plans/sports events
1 Brian			
2 Hazel			
3 Dylan			
4 Matt			

C1

You are going to hear a radio reporter giving the commentary for a match. Look at the words in the box. Which sport are they all connected with? What do they mean?

| umpire | love | game | set | match | serve |

Read the questions, then listen and answer them.

1 What nationality are the players?
2 Who does the reporter expect to win?
3 Why is this an important game?
4 What happens at the end of the game?

C2

Listen again and choose from A, B, C or D to complete the sentences correctly.

1 Rosie Finch is _____ than Lulu Bassett.
   A older   B richer   C fitter   D taller

2 _____ are watching.
   A Rosie's mother and father   C Lulu's manager and husband
   B Rosie's sister and boyfriend   D Lulu's best friend and manager

3 Rosie wins the game because of _____
   A her fast serve.   C her new racquet.
   B her manager's advice.   D her fans.

4 There's a fight because _____
   A the umpire makes a mistake.   C it's a very hot day.
   B Rosie's boyfriend doesn't   D Lulu thinks the umpire is wrong.
     like Lulu's husband.

D

PRONUNCIATION PRACTICE: Singular and plural nouns

You can add an -s to most nouns in English, to make them plural, but there are many where you can't do this, for example, *child, children*. Listen and repeat the singular and plural nouns.

Now listen to some individual words and write S for singular or P for plural.

1 _____	4 _____	7 _____	10 _____	13 _____	16 _____
2 _____	5 _____	8 _____	11 _____	14 _____	17 _____
3 _____	6 _____	9 _____	12 _____	15 _____	18 _____

Final listening tips

1 Try to predict what words you might hear. Think about the topic.
2 Look at the speaker, his or her lips, and his or her body language.
3 Concentrate hard on the speaker's words.
4 If it's a recording, listen again as often as you need to.
5 If it's a live conversation, don't be afraid to ask for help, or ask the speaker to repeat.

PRONUNCIATION BANK

A

Many words sound similar in English. Look at these explanations and see if you can work out what the similar-sounding words are. Then listen and choose the correct explanation of the word you hear.

1 A like *his*, but for a girl
   B opposite of *there*
   C what grows on your head
2 A plural of *was*
   B fighting between countries
   C put on (clothes)
3 A a special shoe for cold or wet weather
   B a small ship, for sailing or rowing
   C paid for
4 A a cook
   B most important
   C opposite of *expensive*

5 A to go away
   B opposite of *death*
   C opposite of *die*
6 A unhappy
   B spoken
   C last letter of the alphabet
7 A a new thought
   B something perfect
   C identity card
8 A longer than a postcard
   B recently
   C opposite of *earlier*

B

You may think you recognise a short word as part of a longer word, but the pronunciation and stress are often different. Look at these pairs of words, then listen and repeat them after the speaker.

please, pleasure   she, shell
cup, cupboard   fat, fatal
pot, potato   car, caravan
hop, hoping   plan, plant

C

Many words in English have silent letters. Listen and circle the silent letters in these words. (Some of the words have more than one silent letter.)

walk   castle
bird   cupboard
thumb   hour
calm   write
why   leopard

Now listen and repeat the words after the speaker.

D

See what a difference one letter can make to the pronunciation of a word! Listen and repeat these words after the speaker.

red, redo	rat, rate	own, gown
sit, site	bath, bathe	mat, mast
mad, made	hall, hallo	cost, coast
lose, loose	face, farce	hot, host

E

Place names often sound quite different from the way they are written. Listen and repeat these place names after the speaker.

Delhi	Durham	Blenheim	Birmingham
Minneapolis	Seattle	Montreal	Reading
Edinburgh	Peterborough	Pittsburgh	Johannesburg
Leicester	Worcester	Gloucester	Bicester
Bournemouth	Houston	Vancouver	Melbourne
Salisbury	Canterbury	Newbury	Shrewsbury
Brighton	Kingston	Wellington	Washington
Norwich	Greenwich	Harwich	Warwick
Yorkshire	Cheshire	Hampshire	Shropshire

F

Here are some more place names from around the world. Listen to the way they are usually pronounced in British English, and repeat them after the speaker.

Argentina	Japan	Egypt	Uruguay
Australia	Europe	the E.U.	the U.S.A.
Dublin	Paris	Florence	Geneva
Moscow	Munich	Berlin	Madrid
Cambridge	Manchester	Glasgow	London
Heathrow Airport	Oxford Circus	the River Thames	Trafalgar Square

G

Look at these words which English has 'borrowed' from other languages. Then listen and repeat them after the speaker.

tycoon	marmalade	yogurt	pyjamas
yacht	garage	hotel	karaoke
sauna	mosquito	carafe	kiosk
chauffeur	duvet	siesta	anorak
macho	tattoo	skiing	bistro

INDEX

PRONUNCIATION

SPEAKING

TAPESCRIPTS

UNIT 1 B

Jane Fletcher: Hello, can I help you?

Teacher: Oh hello. Um, is that, er, Mill House Barns?

JF: It's Mill House *Farm*, but we own the barns, yes.

T: Oh, um, you're the owner, Mrs ...?

JF: Jane Fletcher, Mrs Jane Fletcher, F.L.E.T.C.H.E.R.

T: Right, thanks. Well, I'd like to book a largeish group of students from York High School into the barns for a few nights in July, um, if the price is reasonable.

JF: We charge £4 a night per student.

T: Oh, well that's very good. What does that include exactly?

JF: Well, all the facilities are very basic. The barns are big clean areas, with wooden floors, so there's lots of space to sleep. No bathrooms or hot water of course! Just cold water for washing.

T: I see – a bit of a shock for the students! Um, and what about food?

JF: They do their own cooking. They'll have to bring sleeping bags and their own food with them.

T: Right, it sounds great! Well, I've got 40 students ...

JF: 14, did you say?

T: No, 40. And, um, we'd want to stay for three nights, er, or is it four? No, I was right the first time.

JF: When exactly would this be?

T: From the 17th to the 19th of July, leaving on the 20th.

JF: Yes, we can manage that. What time will you be arriving?

T: Um, oh, it depends. 2.30, I should think. No, er, more like 3 in the afternoon.

JF: It'll cost you £480 then, and we'd like you to pay by cheque, six weeks before you come. York High School, you say? I've put it down in my book.

T: That's fine, it's just what we want. Um, thank you very much, Mrs Fletcher, and I'll be in touch just as soon as ...

UNIT 1 C1

Jerry: How's the quiz coming along, Daisy?

Daisy: Oh dear, Jerry, I haven't even started it yet. Do you feel like helping me with it?

J: General knowledge, is it? Hmm. Um, how many questions do you need?

D: We only need about ten.

J: Well, shall we start with something easy, like who first stepped on the moon? Does everybody know it's Neil Armstrong?

D: They might say Yuri Gagarin or the other American, Buzz Aldrin, mightn't they?

J: Right. And for number 2, how about this – which country has the most TV sets?

D: Oh, that's too easy, it's the USA. Or maybe Japan.

J: Ha! Got you! China's got almost twice as many as the States.

D: Well, I never knew that! OK, now here's one I've thought of – what's the most expensive film ever made?

J: Hmm, no idea. *Titanic*? *Jurassic Park*?

D: *Gone with the Wind* cost a lot to make, too, but actually it's *Titanic* at 250 million dollars.

J: Wow! OK, and question 4 could be on great achievements – who was it who sailed across the Pacific on a raft, a tiny little boat made of wood – remember him?

D: Oh, now who was that? Um, Francis Chichester? Scott of the Antarctic?

J: No, the Norwegian, Thor Heyerdahl.

D: Oh, good, this is coming on well. I know! We could ask how many hairs people have on their heads.

J: About a million, I should think.

D: Actually, it's 100,000. And let's have a sports question for number 6 – who was the youngest ever Wimbledon tennis champion?

J: Must be Boris Becker, or perhaps it was Michael Chang?

D: Wrong! Martina Hingis of Switzerland. She wasn't even 16 when she won the women's doubles. I remember that.

J: Great, now we only need another four.

TAPESCRIPTS

UNIT 1 C2

1 I haven't even started it yet
2 We only need about ten
3 Well, shall we start with
4 like who first stepped on the moon
5 Buzz Aldrin, mightn't they
6 No idea
7 but actually it's *Titanic*
8 Pacific on a raft
9 made of wood – remember him
10 About a million, I should think

UNIT 1 D

six AD
ten sixty-six
eighteen seventy-two
nineteen oh one
nineteen twenty-four
the year two thousand
the twenty-fifth of May
the fourteenth of February
December the eleventh
the first of June
the third of March
a million
a hundred thousand
a thousand
a thousand and one
a hundred and thirty-two
eighty-nine
thirteen   thirty
fifteen   fifty
seventeen   seventy
eighteen   eighty
nineteen   ninety
double five seven two one six
six four three eight oh one
nine four seven three eight six two
five two five eight one three
two nine six oh one seven

UNIT 2 B

1 Hi, Ted, it's Carol here. Just wondered if you felt like coming to the cinema tonight. *Magic Mountain*'s on at the Odeon, and it's had great reviews. It starts at 7.30, so we could meet beforehand for a snack if you like ... at the café in Market Street. Can you ring me back?

2 Ted, this is Donald Ferguson. Meant to ask you at work, but I was too busy with the Brussels project. Um, my wife and I would like to invite you to dinner here one evening. Maybe next week? We were thinking of Friday at about 7. Nothing too formal. I just like to get to know my junior managers a bit better. You can ring me at home.

3 Ted, my old mate, it's Jason here. How's things? And how's that lovely girlfriend of yours, Carol, isn't it? Now why don't you bring her round to my place for a few beers? I've invited a few other people – you may know some of them. Say 8 o'clock Saturday night? Flat 7A, don't forget. See you there!

UNIT 2 C

Sophie: Look, let's sort out a few details for this leaving party of Trevor's, shall we?
Sally: Yes, OK, Sophie. It's quite soon, isn't it?
Sophie: In a couple of weeks' time, the 27th. Now, have you booked the restaurant, Sally?
Sally: No. Oh, I thought you were going to! Oh dear, I am sorry! Um, I'll do it straightaway. Which one did we decide on?
Sophie: Otello's. Better write it down: O. T. E. double L. O. apostrophe S. You know, the one in Spring Street. I hope they can still fit us in.
Sally: Me too! How many of us will there be?
Sophie: Fifteen, all on one big table. We'll want to book the table from about 7.30, I should think.
Sally: OK. Oh, it'll be sad saying goodbye to Trevor, won't it? How long's he been here?
Sophie: For ten years. It's a long time! But we'll give him a good send-off. Tell Otello's we'll want them to do their best!
Sally: Oh yes! Perhaps they could make a special cake, with his name on?
Sophie: Yes, good idea. And after the meal we could go on to a club perhaps, for a bit of dancing.
Sally: Oh yes, that sounds great! But it might mean being a bit late for work the next morning!

UNIT 2 D

1 I'll see you tomorrow.
2 She posted the letter last night.
3 The present? Oh, give it to him!
4 The piano was sold for a hundred pounds.
5 When does the bank close?
6 He'll set the table for you.
7 I bought a really beautiful jacket there.
8 Sit down and have a cup of coffee.

Sentences 1–8 are now repeated.

UNIT 3 B

Woman: You were going to tell me about making soup, weren't you?

Man: Oh, yes, I was. Well, this one's my absolute favourite, and it's *so* easy!

W: It'd better be – I'm not much good at cooking.

M: Aren't you? Oh, well, this is really simple. Let's see – you need a large onion, or a couple of small ones, er, two carrots, a couple of courgettes, a few tomatoes, um, two or three potatoes, and a small piece of chicken. OK? First, cut the chicken up and fry it gently in some oil or butter, in a large pan, for a few minutes.

W: Right.

M: Then chop up the vegetables into small pieces and add them to the chicken. Cook them all together for a bit longer. Keep them moving about with a wooden spoon, so they don't stick and burn. Then add about half a litre of water and bring it to the boil. Add pepper and salt, and turn the heat down.

W: How long do I leave it cooking then?

M: Mmm, 40 minutes to an hour. It makes a really thick, warming, winter soup. If you like, you can sprinkle grated cheese on top, or stir in some yogurt just before serving it.

W: Oh, sounds delicious! I must try it.

UNIT 3 C

Waiter: Would you like to order now, madam?

Customer: Yes, I think I'll have the cream of mushroom soup to start with, please.

W: Cream of mushroom, right.

C: Then I'll have a green salad, er, with a steak, I think.

W: How do you like it done, madam?

C: Oh, medium, thank you.

W: With chips or new potatoes?

C: Chips, please. And I'll have the chocolate pudding – er, no, on second thoughts, the fresh fruit salad afterwards. It's healthier!

W: Yes, quite! Now, anything to drink? Some wine, perhaps?

C: No, just a bottle of mineral water, I think.

W: Thank you, madam. And for you, sir?

UNIT 4 B

Thank you for calling Connex South Central. For general information on train availability and fares, please call National Rail Enquiries on 0345 484950. Please make your selection from the following numbers.

Press 1 for a recorded update on all Connex trains into London. Press 2 if you have any suggestions on the way in which we could improve our services. Press 3 if you wish to purchase or renew a season ticket by credit card. Press 4 for any other information or if you would like to be connected to one of our travel advisers. Please select the number you want now.

UNIT 4 C

Hello, this is National Express. Here are the times of coaches running between Brighton and London. This timetable is valid until the 17th of May. In Brighton arrivals and departures take place at Pool Valley, and in London at Victoria Coach Station. From Mondays to Fridays the first coach leaves Brighton at 6 a.m. and arrives in London at 8.05. Departures after this are at 6.50, arriving at 8.40, and 8.50 arriving at 10.40, and every hour on the hour from 10 a.m. till 9 p.m., arriving one hour 50 minutes later. For the return journey, coaches leave London at 8.45 a.m., arriving in Brighton at 10.35, and then every hour on the half hour from 9.30 a.m. till 10.30 p.m., arriving one hour 50 minutes later. Delays may occur, due to heavy traffic conditions.

At weekends, that is, on Saturdays and Sundays, departures from Brighton take place at 6.20 a.m., arriving at 8.10, and then every hour on the hour from 8 o'clock. Coaches leave London on the half hour every hour from 10.30, arriving one hour 50 minutes later.

A single adult fare is £6, a return is £10 and a day return is £8. Students can travel with a valid student card for £4.50 single, £7.50 return and £6 day return. Children under 14 pay £3 single, £5 return and £4 day return.

To reserve a ticket, please call the National Express reservations number on 0990 010104, or go to your nearest National Express ticket office. Thank you for calling National Express.

UNIT 5 B

1 Hello, this is Ian Rogers, your dentist speaking. Um, I'd just like to know why you missed your appointment *again* last Friday. I'm sure you understand how annoying it is for everyone if people make appointments and then don't turn up. Um, I'd like you to ring me to explain, on 359821, and I'm afraid that if you don't, or I don't find your explanation a very good one, I shall have to charge you £12. Goodbye.

2 Hello darling, it's Mum here. Now how are you? I do hope you're looking after yourself, and eating really well, and not going out too late! I know what you're like! Remember how ill you were last winter. We don't want that to happen again, do we? Now I want you to do two things for me – first, go to bed very early tonight, and second, ring me as soon as you can tomorrow. Have you got my new mobile number? It's 0976 360524. Bye darling!

3 Sylvia, Jenny Smith here. I've wanted to say this for some time, and then I saw you leave early again today, Friday. That's why I'm ringing you at home. You simply can't make a habit of arriving late at work and leaving early. I want you to come and see me about this *first thing* on Monday morning. Don't forget!

4 Good evening, it's Edward Fowles here, F.O.W.L.E.S if you're making a note of it. I'm calling on behalf of the charity, Help The Children. We were wondering if you had any spare time to help us with our work – in our shop, or delivering leaflets or collecting money. Could you ring me back if you are interested? My number's 0181 748 1341. Thank you so much.

UNIT 5 C

1 Er, hi there, it's Guy Bannister here. Just to say I'm supposed to start teaching for you on Monday, but I've got held up here in Moscow. Um, there's a problem with my flight and I'm doing my best, but, er, I won't be arriving until Tuesday. Oh well, there you go! Sorry about that!

2 Hi, this is Susanna Fernandez, your Mexican agent. We have ten students wanting to book the course starting on the 19th, so I hope that'll be all right. They're all advanced level and want to stay for at least six weeks. Can you call or send a fax on the usual number? This is really urgent!

3 Hello, Margareta Svensson speaking. I apologise for not coming to the first week of the intensive course, but my brother is very ill and I must stay with my family. Just one week more and I will come to take your course. Please tell my teacher and say I'm very sorry.

4 Hi, it's Barry here. Oh dear, this is difficult! Um, can you tell the boss I've had a bit of bad luck with the school minibus? Crashed into a car on the way home. I borrowed it over the weekend, to help a friend out, and just went straight into someone. Afraid it's pretty badly damaged. Um, I'm just sorting things out with the police. I'll be in touch later.

UNIT 6 B1

The Hon. Charles: Oh hello, Lucy. I say, isn't this awful about Mother's diamonds?
Lucy: Yes, terrible, Charles! You know, I saw Sir Montague go up to his bedroom at about 6.30. You don't think *he* took them, do you?
C: Oh, I don't think so! He usually dresses for dinner about then. Of course, *I* was in the billiard room, doing some practice, so I didn't see where anyone was. Where were you, by the way?
L: Little me? Oh, I was in the music room all the time. Didn't you hear me on the piano? And the housekeeper – er, what's her name? Mrs Forbes – was in the dining room. Probably making sure everything was in place for dinner. No sign of the butler, though.
C: Morgan? Oh, I know where he was. Mother told me he was in her room for at least half an hour between 6 and 7. They were discussing which wines to have for dinner in the next few days.
L: Ah. And what about Derek? Isn't he gorgeous! Where was he all this time? I heard him go upstairs. I thought perhaps he wanted to talk to your mother.
C: He looked in on me in the billiard room, and mentioned he was going to his room to write a letter. [Ah] Of course, his room's right next door to Mother's! [Oh]

UNIT 6 B2

Mrs Forbes: Well, I don't know, I'm sure! What *is* the world coming to? A thief in this house! Oh, what's going on, do you think, Mr Morgan?
Morgan: I've been butler to Lady Paula for fifteen years, but I have to say she's caused a lot of

problems with this plan of hers for marrying again. It's a pity she didn't stay with Sir Montague – he's a very nice gentleman. But this Derek Donovan! Just after her money, he is, to pay his debts – he owes money to lots of people. She won't be happy with him, I know her well enough to see that. I heard Sir Montague say once that their divorce was all a misunderstanding, and they should get back together again. He's very jealous of Derek Donovan.

Mrs F: Oh, dear, dear! And you can see that Lucy Bisto's in love with Charles. [Yeah] I think she really hates Lady Paula because she doesn't allow her son much money. That's what Miss Lucy thinks.

M: And we all know Charles owes a lot of money himself. He likes going to casinos and horse-racing too much!

Mrs F: Oh, poor Lady Paula! I know what it's like to have family problems – there's my son who's still in trouble with the police. [Oh] It *is* a worry.

M: I can see that, Mrs Forbes. But Derek Donovan's the real problem. Think how comfortable we'd be if life just went on the same, and Lady Paula didn't remarry!

UNIT 6 C

1 cot, cut   got, gut   gone, gun   shot, shut   cop, cup   not, nut   choc, chuck

Have a cup of coffee? With some nuts, or some chocolate?
Bob lost his job, and had to cut his costs.
Tom shut up shop, and chucked the key in a bucket.
He's got a lot of bottle, but the cops have gone for him with their guns!

2 pet, pat   men, man   Ben, ban   letter, latter   said, sad   met, mat   pen, pan

The men banned Pat from using her pen.
The cat sat on the mat and Ben penned a letter.
Ben patted his pet and said sadly, 'I've never met a cat like you!'

UNIT 7 B

1 Me? Exercise? You must be joking, pal! I wouldn't be seen dead in a leotard, or whatever the thing's called! No! I'd rather hang out with my mates watching telly and that. There's some good programmes on, you know.

2 Well, I swim every day after school and at weekends in the local pool. I have to, 'cause I'm in the Kent under 18s, and the whole team has to practise a lot. I like it, it's good for you. And you never know, I might get to the Olympics one day.

3 Me and my friends, we do step or aerobics twice a week at the sports centre. It only costs £2 a session for students, so it's cheap really. And it's good fun! You feel great afterwards, really warm and fit.

4 All my life I've been keen on football. I go to watch matches whenever I can. Last year I played for the school team, but I'm not good enough this year. I'd like to be as good as Ronaldo. It's a great game.

5 I think I must be what they call a chocoholic. I really love the stuff. I can eat a whole box of chocolates in about ten minutes! It's awful, isn't it? But I've tried to stop eating chocolate and I simply can't!

TAPESCRIPTS

UNIT 7 C

Presenter: Now I'm delighted to welcome Dr Holly O'Neill to the studio today. She's going to give us a few tips on keeping fit and healthy. Over to you, Dr O'Neill.

Dr O'Neill: Thank you, Ryan. Well, I'd like to start by saying how important it is to eat properly. So many people miss out breakfast completely, or just have a coffee and a bit of bread, and that really isn't a good idea. Others don't eat anything during the day, and then have a very big, heavy meal at night, just before going to bed. That isn't good for you, either. No, the best thing is to eat regular, small meals throughout the day. And don't add any salt to your food – it isn't necessary. And drink lots of water as well. Tea and coffee don't really help at all. Try to eat all sorts of things, to give your body a variety of proteins, minerals, vitamins and so on. Fruit and vegetables are especially good – eat at least five portions a day. You'll feel much better for it, I promise you!

P: Sorry, *five*, did you say? That sounds a lot.

Dr O'N: Well, you'll get used to it. Then there's the question of exercise. Different people need different amounts of this, but a good general rule is to make sure you exercise *regularly*, perhaps two or three times a week. It can be walking or swimming or football or aerobics, whatever you like doing. You have to enjoy it, otherwise you'll give it up. Leave the car at home if you can, and *walk* to the post office or the shops – it's cheaper! Doing your own housework and gardening is pretty good exercise, too. Well, that's it for today. Tomorrow I'll be talking about stress and how *that* affects our health.

P: Well, thank you, Dr O'Neill. We'll remember all that and we'll look forward to hearing your tips on dealing with stress tomorrow.

UNIT 8 B

1 Look, I *really* am sorry I forgot to book the tickets. I know you really wanted to go to the concert, and now it's probably too late. But maybe I could ring the box office and see if anyone's returned their tickets. I am *so* sorry ...

2 How do you do? You're working with the Professor, aren't you? I'm delighted to meet you. Of course I've read about your work in the scientific journals – some *most* interesting ideas that I'd love you to ...

3 In the first few months of the new government, a great effort was made to improve the economy. Public spending was cut and there were no pay rises at all, so as a result many people went to work abroad and found ...

4 Look, I'm tired of this. It makes me absolutely furious! How many times have I told you to photocopy the reports *first*! And another thing, you still haven't filed them correctly!

5 I just don't know what to do! You *must* help me! I'm in terrible trouble! They'll be so angry with me when they find out! What am I going to do?

UNIT 8 C

Well, my name's Wang Chen and I speak several languages fluently – Malay, because my dad's Malaysian, Mandarin Chinese, because my mother's Chinese, and English, because I was sent to an English school, in Kuala Lumpur, the capital of Malaysia. That's where we live. I speak a little Arabic, too, and a bit of German. I think the language I like best is Chinese, because that's what I speak with all my friends. I suppose I'm best at speaking Malay, but when it comes to writing I'm much better at English than anything else. I really want to travel to other countries in the future, then my German, Arabic and English will all get better. Listening's usually the big problem for me – people speak so fast!

UNIT 8 D

1 She's been here for ages.
2 I've never seen such a pretty cottage before.
3 You haven't been to Berlin yet, have you?
4 He isn't one of your friends, is he?
5 We're staying for about two days.
6 Here's the letter. I hope you'll give it to him as soon as you can.

she's   I've   haven't   isn't   we're   here's   you'll

Sentences 1–6 are now repeated.

UNIT 9 B

1 Er, hello, could you give me a price, please, on a return flight to Toronto? Yes, in Canada! It would be next Monday or Tuesday, and coming back a week later. *How* much? £450! Isn't that rather expensive? Is that a scheduled or a charter flight? Scheduled, oh, I see. OK, thanks, I'll think about it.

2 Hello, I'd just like to confirm my flight home. My name's Johnson, and it's flight BY254A, leaving Corfu at 3.25 on Saturday the 23rd. Is that OK? No last-minute changes or delays? Oh, great! Thanks, bye.

3 Morning, here's my ticket. Ah, and you want the passport, too, don't you? Er, just this suitcase to check in. It's not all that heavy. Um, a no-smoking seat, please, by the window if possible. What time are we boarding? 11.15, I see. And which gate number? Five. OK, thanks.

4 We've finally decided on the Air France flight please, if it's still available. Uh-huh, that's for two of us, going out on Friday morning. What was the time again? Hmm, 9.45, with half an hour check-in. Yes, that's right. Yes? Two seats left, oh, wonderful! I'll give you my Visa card number now, shall I? Right, here goes ...

UNIT 9 C

Flight number BA2724 to Stockholm now boarding at Gate 29, due to depart at 10.20. All passengers for the Stockholm flight please go to Gate 29. Passengers for Pisa on flight number EAF3310 should go to Gate 32, that's Gate 32, where your plane is waiting for you. Departure time scheduled for 10.22.
Flight number AF8728 to Riga has been delayed and will now depart at 12.15. Passengers for Riga please wait in the departure lounge. You will be boarding at Gate number 11.
Flight number KGC934 to Madrid is now boarding at Gate 15 and will be taking off at 11.05. Please go to Gate 15 to start boarding now.
Passengers for Lisbon, Athens and Bonn, please wait in the lounge. Flight number MON692 to Lisbon is due to take off at 11.10. Flight number CA5541 to Athens will take off at 11.25, and flight number LH973 to Bonn has a scheduled time of 11.30. Gate numbers will be announced shortly.

UNIT 10 B

Hello, this is the Grand Theatre in Wexham. This week we are delighted to present the Royal Shakespeare Company in William Shakespeare's well-known play, *A Midsummer Night's Dream*. The play will run from Tuesday to Saturday. There will be a matinee performance starting at 2.30 on Thursday and Saturday afternoons, while evening shows start at 7.45 every night. Prices range from £8 for gallery seats, to our top price of £22 for the royal circle seats.
Next week, for three nights only, we are proud to present *A Woman In White*, adapted from the Wilkie Collins novel, and performed by the New London Theatre. This will start at 8 p.m. on Wednesday, Thursday and Saturday. Prices are from £7 to £18.
If you wish to book tickets for either of these plays, please press 1 on your phone, and have your credit card ready, or ring the box office on 01752 348348. Thank you for calling the Grand Theatre, Wexham.

UNIT 10 C

Harry: Hi Adam, do you fancy seeing a film tonight?
Adam: OK, yes, why not? With you and Ellie, you mean? What's on?
Ellie: Well, you two won't like it, but I really want to see *Hope Floats*.
H: Oh, not again, Ellie! You've already seen it three times! You must know every word by heart!
E: Look, it's my kind of film, all right? It's what I like. Romantic, and so sad, you know. Makes me cry.
A: Well, OK, but Harry and me, we don't go for the love interest, do we, Harry? I have a feeling *Manhattan*'s on, actually – that's Woody Allen's best, I think. I'm a real fan of his. He's so funny! What do you think, Harry?
H: Yes, that's a good one. Or how about *Blade*? It's supposed to be a brilliant horror movie, full of vampires and the undead, you know the kind of thing. Really scary! How about it, Ellie?
E: Who wants to be scared? You know I really hate horror films. I just never believe in any of that ghostly stuff. Isn't there *anything* we can agree on?
A: Maybe we should just go for a coffee instead.
H: Yeah, maybe you're right.
E: Yeah, OK, why not?

UNIT 11 B

Mr Cage: 561224.
Julia Hills: Hello, is that Mr Cage?
Mr C: Yes, speaking.
JH: Oh, I'm Julia Hills. I saw your advertisement in the Evening Echo – you know, for your flat in Edward Road.
Mr C: Oh yes, you're interested in that, are you? Well, it's a very nice flat, I can tell you. Large, sunny, central heating – it's even got a south-facing balcony!
JH: Oh really? It sounds lovely. Um, is it expensive?
Mr C: Not at all, no. I only charge a hundred pounds a week. Plus all the bills, of course. You wouldn't expect the rent to include gas and electricity, would you?
JH: Oh – oh no, I suppose not. But that's still a bit more than I, um, I don't earn very much, you see.
Mr C: I think you'll want the flat when you see it. Better come round and have a look. There's a lovely little kitchen.
JH: Is it, er, self-contained?
Mr C: Oh yes. You have your own front door, you know. You can come and go as you like, and invite friends round. Much better than just a room in someone's house.
JH: It does sound good. Can I perhaps see it tonight? I might bring my brother along with me.
Mr C: Fine! Shall we say 7.30ish? I can meet you there – it's number 30A, with a yellow door.
JH: Right, thanks very much. See you then.

UNIT 11 C

Grant: Sharon, I think we should think about doing some decorating soon, you know. We've been here five years now and the place still looks a mess!
Sharon: Yes, I know, love. You're right. But there's been so much else to do. [Mmm.] Where do you think we should start?
G: Well, how about painting the living room? I really think we should throw away that horrible old brown carpet, too, and get a new one.
S: Well, I think I'd rather start with the bathroom. I hate those pink walls! And the shower's not working properly any more, you know. It's getting quite urgent.
G: Yes, you're right about the shower. I don't know. Perhaps this room's more important to start

with. Look how dirty these walls are around the cooker. We could paint everything white, I suppose.
S: Oh, but what about the bedroom, though? It really needs some new wallpaper. And new curtains.
G: I don't know – I think we're going to have to get someone in to help us. We can't do all this ourselves. We just haven't got the time.
S: You're right. Let's get someone in.

UNIT 11 D

chair, share   watch, wash   cheese, she's
choose, shoes   catch, cash   match, mash
chip, ship   cheap, sheep

Watch out! You'll fall off that chair!
Is she really choosing those shoes?
Shall we share the cash, and watch the match?

thick, sick   worth, worse   think, sink
thumb, some   mouth, mouse
although, also   that, sat

This fog is so thick – it's worse than I thought!
The child put her thumb rather thoughtfully into
    her mouth.
They sat there, thinking beautiful thoughts about
    something.

UNIT 12 B

1
A: Freeman and Peabody. Can I help you?
B: I hope so. I'm ringing to tell you I've got a serious problem with the microwave I bought from your store yesterday.
A: Oh, really, madam? What kind of problem?
B: Well, absolutely nothing happens when you switch it on. It's so annoying!
A: I see. Have you kept the receipt?
B: Oh yes. I've got it here. Look, this just isn't good enough. I'll have to come all the way back into town with it. And the parking is terrible! It really is too bad.
A: Mmm, I'm very sorry, madam, but naturally we'll refund your money, if you return the item to us with the receipt, and of course there is a ...

2
A: Hi, Janet, how are things?
B: Oh guess what, it's brilliant, I've got the job!
A: Oh, that's marvellous! When did you hear?
B: Oh, just today. I can't believe it, it's so fantastic!

I'll be living in Paris, just imagine!
A: Lucky you! So when can we come and stay?

3
A: The thing is, officer, she's never stayed out this late before, and I really can't imagine where she is. I just keep thinking ...
B: Now, don't worry, Mrs Jenkins, we'll do our best. When did you see her last?
A: Well, it was at 7 o'clock when she set out to meet her friends. She said she'd be back at ten, her usual time, but I've waited and waited, and it's so unlike her to be late ...

UNIT 12 C

1 It's new, you see, and it's a bit tricky, but it's easy once you get the idea. To lock it, just push the handle upwards. When you want to open it, put the key in and turn it to the right, then push down on the handle.

2 They are complicated to use properly, unless you've worked with them a lot. But getting started is simple. Look, first of all, just plug it in, switch on at the plug, and switch on here at the front of the screen. Let it warm up a bit, and then type something on the keyboard!

3 It's wonderful. I don't know what I'd do without it. You press this button here to open the drawer. Well, OK, switch on the power first! Pop the disk in, and tell it to play. Just lie back and enjoy!

4 It works really well. Just put it round the top of the jar, make sure it's tight, then pull one end of the rubber gently, while holding the handle. The lid'll come off in no time!

UNIT 13 B

George: Look, you say what you think we should get, Zoë, and I'll write it down.
Zoë: I think we should have a roast chicken, and different sorts of salad, and very cold white wine, and lots of fruit like melon and peaches.
G: Hang on a minute! We've got to carry it all, remember! And peaches aren't even in the shops yet! No, let's stick to something simple like, um, sandwiches and crisps.
Z: What! That's not very exciting for a picnic. I tell you what – we can do roast chicken *and* sandwiches with lots of different fillings.

G: OK, that's great! Now, er, what shall I put on my list – bread, butter, um, some nice cheese?
Z: Yes, and tomatoes. What about a lettuce?
G: No need, there's one in my fridge. But we must have a cucumber, um, carrots, radishes, oh, and mayonnaise. Oh, wait till you taste my special salad sandwiches!
Z: Gosh, I can't wait! Now, have you put a *large* chicken on the list? And we need some eggs – we can hard-boil them and make egg mayonnaise.
G: Oh yes! What about a tin of tuna? And some olives, um, and some slices of beef?
Z: Yes, and a packet of pasta. Then I could make a pasta salad with some tuna and olives. Everybody likes that.
G: And a bottle of salad dressing, you know, sort of oil and vinegar mixture.
Z: Mmm. Now, what else do we need? Oh yes, the drinks! There are a lot of us, remember. Some bottles of white wine ...
G: And a few cartons of fruit juice.
Z: Brilliant! And lots and lots of strawberries – *they're* in the shops now!

UNIT 13 C

Well, it all started when I decided to buy my girlfriend a sweater for her birthday. Like so many things, it seemed a good idea at the time! I went straight into town, to one of the big department stores, you know, and bought her a lovely red sweater. I thought she'd love it, but you never can tell, can you? She took one look at it and said, 'I just don't see myself in red!' and that was that! So I had to take it back to the shop to change it, and this time I got her a blouse, not red, of course, a rather nice green, actually. I gave it to her that evening, but when she took it out of the bag, she burst into tears and said, 'Do you really think I'm as large as that?' It certainly did look rather big when she held it up – I must have got the wrong size. Anyway, I was going to take it back to the shop and change it, but I happened to be talking to the girl next door, and she saw the bag and asked what was in it, and when I told her, she asked to try it on. And she loved it! So I gave it to her. And when my girlfriend saw her wearing the green blouse, she refused to see me ever again. So, that's how I started going out with the girl next door!

UNIT 14 B

Did I ever tell you about the time I bumped into my brother in New York? No? Well, it was really amazing! All this happened 25 years ago, actually. Seems ages, doesn't it? Yes, I'd, um, I'd just finished university and I decided to go to the States for three months in the summer. I really wanted to find out about American culture, get to know American people, and earn some money, as well as having a holiday. In those days you could work for six weeks in the States and then travel for six weeks on a special visa. So I got a job looking after someone's children in New York – that's another story! Did that for a month and a half, then started on my travels.

The cheapest thing was to travel by Greyhound – you know, long-distance coaches. From New York I went to Washington DC, and then down to Atlanta in Georgia – had some friends there. Then to New Orleans – that must be my absolutely favourite place – the food is simply wonderful, and so is the nightlife! Then over to Los Angeles, and the Grand Canyon. I walked all the way down and all the way up. Had to have a rest day after that! I even went to Las Vegas to see the casinos, but I didn't do any gambling – I was being very careful with my money by then. Then on to San Francisco, which is a lovely city, very hilly but beautiful. Rather strange and interesting people on the West Coast!

From there I headed inland via Kansas City – that's in what's called the Mid-West – miles of rolling dusty plains, with not much happening, but the nicest people. I stayed with a friend I'd met in Geneva the year before. And then to Chicago, a quick look at the Great Lakes, and back to New York for my flight home. This is where the funny thing happened.

I was walking down the corridor of this cheap little student hotel – I had to stay just one night in New York to catch my plane the next day – when guess who I saw walking towards me – my brother! I had no idea he was coming to the States, and he and I had picked the same hotel, just for one night, thousands of miles from home! And guess what the first thing he said to me was? 'Clare! Great to see you! Can you lend me $100?' Typical little brother! It was lucky for him that he'd met me and I had some spare cash, as he and his friends had almost nothing left. He paid me back later, I think. Or did he? I'm not sure. Wasn't it funny though, seeing him ...?!

UNIT 14 C

Well, you wouldn't believe how awful it was! I mean it's not as if it was cheap. It cost us a fortune! £3,000 for the two of us, and Barbara really thinks we should get some of our money back. I mean, Travel International is supposed to be a good company, isn't it? Well, that's what Barbara thought. A good thing we were only there for ten days. For a start, our room was really small, and the bathroom wasn't cleaned every day! Can you believe it? The Shelton at Hyderabad is a 5-star hotel. That's what it said in the brochure anyway. Haven't you heard of it? And the food, well it was just too hot and spicy. Barbara and I like our food mild, you know. The breakfast – well, they didn't give us any more than coffee and toast. And Barbara likes a little more than that in the mornings! You know, cereal, couple of eggs, you know the sort of thing. The service was terrible! And do you know, when Barbara told the waiters how slow they were, they were very rude to her! Well, we didn't even think much of the excursions, because they just put us on a coach, with no tour guide, and even worse, no lunch! They did say we'd get breakfast, lunch and dinner included every day, and really, when you pay that sort of money, Barbara says she's going to have ...

UNIT 14 D

sit, seat   dip, deep   hill, heal   chip, cheap
   hit, heat   fill, feel   wick, weak
got, goat   rod, road   Tod, toad   doll, dole
   mop, mope   hop, hope
fat, fate   hat, hate   mac, make   back, bake
   sack, sake   rack, rake
lit, light   bit, bite   mitt, might   hit, height
   Brit, bright   sit, sight

UNIT 15 B

1

Megan: Joshua, hello there! How lovely to see you! Haven't seen you for ages!

Joshua: Megan, hi! Um, you're right, must be, oh, I don't know, five years? Saw you last at that Rome conference, didn't I?

M: Oh gosh, yes. I'd forgotten about that. So, what have you been doing lately?

J: Well, the company moved me to head office in Seattle and then moved me right back again. So, not sure where I'll be next year. Look, I really gotta go, but, no, let's ... let's meet for a proper talk, shall we? I'll give you a call – very soon OK?

2

Boss: Come in, Nathan, I want you to meet someone. Er, Jack, do you know Nathan Oliver, our new marketing assistant? Jack Bennett, Nathan Oliver.

Jack/Nathan: How do you do?

Boss: Jack's our Head of Production, Nathan. I think he was on holiday when you were being interviewed. That's why you haven't met before. Now, er, let's sit down and have a chat about this idea of yours, Nathan. I think Jack will be very interested in it. Go on, Nathan.

N: Oh, well, um, you see, Mr Bennett, I was on the phone the other day to one of our best customers and, er, and he said why don't we ...

3

Emma: Rebecca, hi, here I am!

Rebecca: Where have you been, Emma? I've been waiting here in the rain for ages!

E: Oh, *so* sorry I'm late – I got stuck in a traffic jam. The bus just didn't move at all!

R: Why didn't you get out and walk?

E: It was miles away! But I really am sorry. Why didn't you wait inside? You're terribly wet!

R: Because you got the times wrong! The cinema's closed, that's why! It doesn't open for another half an hour!

4

Man 1: That was really delicious, wasn't it?

Man 2: Mmm, yes. We must come here again. Great to catch up on all the news like this.

M1: Absolutely. Now remember – come and stay with us any time. My parents would love to see you.

M2: Ah, that is kind. I certainly will. Look, I'll just call the waiter and pay the bill.

M1: No, no, it's *my* turn to pay! You paid last time, remember? I insist.

M2: Oh well, thanks very much! I did enjoy it.

M1: Good ...

UNIT 15 C

Rachel: Oh hello. We haven't met before, have we?

Charlie: No, I ... I don't think so. I'm Charlie Bywater. And you are ...?

R: Oh, I'm Rachel, Rachel McDonald. Are you a friend of Annette's?

C: Yes, I used to work with her actually, at Prada, but then I changed jobs.

R: Oh? What do you do now, then?

C: Well, I'm a leather buyer for Gucci. I travel all over the world finding the right sort of leather for our jackets.

R: Wow! Do you? I like the sound of all that travelling! I work in a lab all day.

C: Oh really! What do you do?

R: Well, I'm a food scientist and I work for Cadbury's. I have to try out new recipes and flavours, and taste all the new kinds of chocolate, to make sure customers are going to like them.

C: Hmm. Must be great getting all that free chocolate!

R: Well, actually, I used to love chocolate, but now I can't stand it. I don't even like the smell!

C: Oh, let me get you another drink – um, tomato juice, was it ...?

UNIT 15 D

1 Yes, I used to work with her actually, at Prada
2 Oh really, what do you do?
3 Well, actually, I used to love chocolate.
4 Let me get you another drink – tomato juice was it?

Sentences 1–4 are now repeated.

UNIT 16 B

Welcome to the Queen's House in Greenwich, south of the River Thames in London. This was the first neo-classical building in Britain, and was designed by the architect Inigo Jones, who was greatly influenced by Italian architecture. The house was built for Queen Anne of Denmark, wife of King James I, and building went on between 1616 and 1635, when it was finally completed.

You are in the Great Hall. Note the black and white marble floor and the splendid oak Gallery. Go up the round staircase, walk along the Gallery and turn right into the King's Stateroom. This is the most richly furnished room in the house, with a large number of royal portraits. Continue into the King's Waiting Room, where visitors had to wait before seeing the king, and then into the Library, where he used to read. From there, the next room is the King's Bedroom, a large corner room overlooking the park, with his Bathroom next door, and after that, his Study, quite a small room near the staircase. Walk through the large central room, the Dining Room, to reach the Gallery again, overlooking the Great Hall.

Now you are going into the Queen's part of the house. Turn left into the Queen's Stateroom, a room almost as large as the King's Stateroom. Note the luxurious coverings on the walls, the chairs and the bed. This room was used by Queen Anne, and later by King Charles I's Queen, Henrietta Maria. Continue into the narrow Queen's Waiting Room, and then into the Music Room, and finally into the Queen's Bedroom, just like the King's, with a Bathroom next door, and then a Maid's Room next to that. From the Maid's Room you can go out onto the balcony for a view of Greenwich Park, or go downstairs again.

UNIT 16 C

Marion: Now, wasn't that nice, Fred? A really beautiful house!

Fred: Don't see why it's called the *Queen's* House. It's got *King's* rooms in it, hasn't it? So why don't they call it the *King's* House?

M: Oh, Fred, don't you ever listen? It was built for Queen Anne of Denmark – that's why it's the *Queen's* House. Very nice of her to let the King come and visit, I'm sure. Now, what shall we go and see next?

F: I'm not going anywhere! My feet hurt.

M: Oh come on, Fred! We only come to London once a year! There's all this afternoon before our train home. Um, how about a nice boat trip on the River Thames? Or we could do a bit of shopping in Oxford Street.

F: No! I'm not going shopping! You spend enough time doing that at home. Oh, if we have to do something, it might as well be the boat trip, I suppose. How much does it cost?

M: Oh, very cheap, don't let's worry about that. And afterwards we could get on a bus and go to Trafalgar Square. They do a lovely pot of tea in the National Gallery restaurant. You'd like that.

F: Oh, all right then. But I warn you, next year I'm staying at home. You can go to London on your own!

UNIT 16 D

1 hello hair Harry his hers happy hurry horse haunted house

Harry's on holiday in Honolulu in a haunted house.
Have you heard, horse-riding makes Helen happy?

2 rough tough enough
thorough borough
thought bought sought fought
cough through

I thought I'd bought a tough pair of shoes.
She coughed all through the night.
It's a rough borough to live in.

UNIT 17 B

Thank you for calling Little Stoke Manor, where our new programme of activities will be starting in four weeks' time. We have an intensive weekend of French, or you could choose Portuguese. And this year, for the first time, we are offering intensive Russian or Japanese. These are all lined up for the first weekend in May, with a week's course on Writing Short Stories to follow, taught by that wonderful writer David Malcolm, and then, starting on the 1st of June, our one-to-one tennis coaching with Alistair Ridley, lasting for two weeks. Next on the programme is a weekend course on finding out about your family history, led by Lizzie Windrush, whose own family has been a fascinating study. That's on the 6th and 7th of June. Next is our very popular yoga course, running every Tuesday and Thursday for six weeks from the 9th of June – the teacher is Annabel Vickers, as usual. And then another weekend course, this time on Understanding the Internet, with our computer expert, Dave Smith, on the 13th and 14th of June. Finally, we have our summer course on Modern Art, taught by our old friend Peter Dennis, for the last two weeks of June. We do hope there's something of interest to you. If so, please ring 0191 4876315 to book your place on a course. Thank you.

UNIT 17 C

Melissa: Scott, have you got those leaflets about health clubs you were looking at the other day?
Scott: You mean the fitness centres? Yeah, sure. Er, they're here somewhere – oh, here they are.
M: Let's have a look then. Oh, this one looks good. Only £15 a month! That's cheap, isn't it? Sweatshop, it's called. That's a good name!
S: Well, but what facilities has it got, Mel? That's the important thing.
M: Yeah, you're right. Um, a gym, of course, and weights. That's all. But it's in the town centre. Have you got a pen? Can you jot down the phone number for me? It's 772438.
S: 772438 … got that. What about the others? *You* might need more than just a gym to get fit!
M: Do you mind, you cheeky thing! You're the one who needs to get fit! Anyway, we decided we'd go together, right? No, this one looks better – it's called Body Matters. It's got a gym *and* a pool, and they do yoga, too. It's £180 a year. How much is that a month? Oh, wait a minute – it's the same price as Sweatshop! It's near the station, so you could come in on the train. Here's the number. It's 413992.
S: 413992, right. Yes, that sounds great, but maybe this one's worth a look. See what you think. It's called Fitness First, and it's out of town, but they do have a free car park, so you could give me a lift, couldn't you?
M: I might. Depends if you're nice to me.
S: I'm always nice to you. It's got tennis courts, a sauna, a big pool and aerobics classes. But it's £250 a year. I think that's too much, don't you?
M: Yeah! Let's look at Body Matters again. At least it's more reasonable …

UNIT 18 B

Sam: Alice, did I ever tell you about the time I capsized in the Irish Sea?
Alice: No, you didn't, Sam! What happened?
S: Well, it was probably the most dangerous thing that's ever happened to me. You know my boat?
A: Yes, oh yes.
S: Well, this was, er, ooh, a couple of summers ago. I was sailing the yacht from North Wales up through the Irish Sea to the west coast of Scotland. [Uh huh] Er, my girlfriend was on board – oh, you know Natasha, don't you?
A: Natasha, oh yes.
S: And a friend of mine, Jake, er, he's about 45, and his 16-year-old son, Tod. [Ooh] Just the four of us. It was beautiful weather, but the Irish Sea can be a bit rough, so we were all on deck. [Mmm] Anyway, we were just off the coast of Northern Ireland, when suddenly …
A: Oh no, what happened?
S: Wait for it! The boat just hit a wave and turned on its side, [Oh] and then right over! [Oh, no] We couldn't believe it! We were all thrown out immediately.
A: Oh no!
S: Luckily we were all wearing life-jackets …
A: Yes!
S: And when we surfaced, we managed to swim back to the boat. We couldn't get it the right way up, though – it's very difficult to do if you're in the water. [Mmm] Natasha and Tod climbed on top and sat there, while Jake and I held on for dear life.
A: Oh, how awful!
S: There we were, in the middle of the sea, miles from land, with no way of calling for help. As I said, it was a warm summer day, but even so, the water was very cold, [Oh] and I was beginning to think it was the end, when suddenly we saw the Irish ferry. [Ooh] It goes from Larne to Stranraer on the Scottish coast, and it had seen us. We were *so* lucky! [Wow] The captain turned the ferry off its normal course, and picked us up. Honestly, they were *so* nice to us. [Oh] Wrapped us up in blankets and gave us hot drinks and spare clothes, and took us to Stranraer.
A: Oh, what a relief! Weren't you lucky!
S: Oh yes. We were even on the local TV news, you know! [Oh, oh] Then, of course, we had to get home by train, and arrange for someone to get the boat, but that's another story.
A: Well, I can imagine …

UNIT 18 C

Woman: Did you know, I've just booked our tickets for New Zealand?
Man: No, really? Oh, how fabulous! You'll love it!
W: Yes, I'm sure we will. The thing is, I thought you could give me a few tips – you know, if there's anything we ought to avoid, or take with us, that sort of thing.
M: Ah, let me see. Well, there are a couple of things. You see, it's one of the safest countries to travel in, and the people are really helpful and friendly, but there's quite a bit of wildlife. I mean, sharks swim off the beaches, you know.
W: Oh dear! Do they actually attack people?
M: No, hardly ever. But if you come face to face with one when you're diving, the best thing is just to swim quietly away. [Mmm] Ah, and with jellyfish, it's a good thing to avoid them if you can. They can sting you quite badly.
W: Oh dear! What else is there to look out for?
M: Well, there's a nasty little spider that's poisonous. You probably won't actually die if it bites you ...
W: Oh, that's a relief!
M: But you'll have to go to hospital. It has a shiny black body with a red patch on, so watch out for that.
W: We might do a bit of camping, so we'll have to be careful where we put our tent.
M: Yes, and the other thing is that you shouldn't really leave anything valuable lying around in your car. You know I was there last summer? [Mmm] Well, my suitcase was stolen from the back of the car, [Oh] with my jacket, and radio, and camera. It made life pretty difficult for a few days! But that kind of thing can happen anywhere when you're travelling.
W: Oh, yes. We'll take out insurance anyway, of course.
M: Mmm. You must be really looking forward to it. It's the most beautiful ...

UNIT 18 D

1 I'd never been there.
2 It's later than I thought.
3 They've planted two apple trees.
4 The flight takes five hours.
5 We'll have to pay the bills this week.
6 She's bought a cottage in the country.
7 You'll always be welcome.
8 She's a very good writer.
9 What a lovely day!
10 He often arrives late.

Sentences 1–10 are now repeated.

UNIT 19 B

Jessica: So, what exactly do you do, Amy?
Amy: Well, I'm a farm accountant. You know I drive round visiting farms?
J: Well, yes.
A: Well, I help farmers with their accounts. [Oh] It's all to do with money coming in and going out, taxes, expenses and so on. You see, they're so busy, they don't have time for all the paperwork.
J: Oh, it must be really lovely being out in the country, driving round all those beautiful lanes, while I'm stuck in my office!
A: Well, it's great in the summer, especially on a sunny morning with all the birds singing. But it's quite a different story in the winter. The roads can get quite dangerous if there's a lot of snow or if it freezes. I nearly had an accident this morning on an icy bend. [Oh] But people in the country will always stop and help you.
J: So, you wouldn't want to work in town?
A: No, definitely not. I like being able to breathe fresh air and see green fields on my way to work. I love the open space and the sense of freedom.

UNIT 19 C

Patsy: Hi, Rory! Did you have a nice weekend?
Rory: Oh hi, Patsy. Yes, it was good.
P: What did you do?
R: Well, there was nothing on in the village, as usual. So we got the bus into Bristol on Saturday night. The big city!
P: Oh. Where did you go?
R: We went to that new theatre in Gladstone Street. Have you been there?
P: No, not yet. How long's it been open?
R: Oh, about a month or so. There was a really good comedy on. A friend of mine saw it at the Edinburgh Festival.
P: Oh, brilliant! Did you go somewhere afterwards?
R: Yes. The play finished about half ten and we were supposed to get the last bus back to Winterbourne at eleven, but it was such a good atmosphere – it was so long since I'd been in town on a Saturday night – that we just walked round for

a bit. There were loads of people on the streets. And then we ended up in a little bar – the Café Prague – where they had live music. They stay open pretty late. So we had to get a taxi back in the end.

P: I bet that cost a bit!

R: Yes, it was pretty expensive. But it was a great evening, so it was worth it.

P: You should do it more often.

UNIT 19 D

1 Are you sure it's number 2?
2 Did you lock the door?
3 Is there a shop that sells milk?
4 Do *you* always walk the dog?
5 Do you live near the school?
6 Has he lived there for long?
7 Are you on holiday next week?
8 Is it the first today?
9 Did they come by bus?
10 Have you seen the doctor yet?

11 How are you today?
12 Can you swim?
13 What's your name?
14 Have you got a bike?
15 Where does she live?
16 Why are you late?
17 Have you got any pets?
18 Do you speak Arabic?
19 How much did that cost?
20 Do you like him?

Sentences 11–20 are now repeated.

UNIT 20 B

1 I would like to teach more, but it's really difficult with my two very small children. So I find it works pretty well, just teaching in the mornings. Then I can spend time with them in the afternoon.

2 It's quite different from being at school. Er, I live away from home now, and I have to manage my own money. But I like the freedom of it, oh yes …

3 The uniforms are so expensive, that's the worst thing. But Nick and Christina do like the school, so at least we don't have to force them to go off there every morning. They take sandwiches – it's cheaper than school lunches.

4 In my day, pupils were very polite and always said, 'Good morning, Mrs Nichols,' and, you know, opened the door for you and so on. I'm glad I'm not teaching any more – too old for it these days.

5 It's fun when our teacher reads us stories in the afternoon, after lunch, and I like it when we play games. But sometimes the lessons are a bit difficult and I need extra help.

UNIT 20 C

Liam: Jade! Where are you off to?

Jade: Ah, I'm going over to the bookshop. I've just got time before my next lecture.

L: You don't even have to go to the lecture, do you?

J: Well, no, if I didn't go, nobody would notice. There are too many of us for that. And anyway, nobody minds, as long as we do all our reading.

L: I can't believe it! Things are so relaxed for you arts people. We poor scientists are stuck in our labs from nine to five. Do you realise, we *have* to be there?

J: Oh, bad luck, Liam! But you do get an hour off for lunch!

L: Huh! I think I work twice as hard as you do.

J: Ah, but don't forget, we go on reading and studying and worrying all over the weekend, when your labs are closed.

L: Well, I must say, I haven't noticed *you* doing much of that. What about last weekend, then? You were at Ricky's party, weren't you …?

UNIT 20 D

1 interesting telephone awfully letter secretary sandwich finish project

2 potato tomato ridiculous amusing employer banana graffiti reporter

3 weekend hotel shampoo engineer mayonnaise kangaroo referee

The secretary received an awfully interesting letter from her employer.

The engineer spent a quiet weekend in a hotel, before finishing his project.

Would you like mayonnaise in your tomato sandwich?

UNIT 21 B1

Well, it's my boyfriend Lewis I'm worried about. I mean, we've been going out for two months now, and he doesn't really talk to me! He's the strong, silent type, I suppose, fantastically good looking, but he's never said much, and lately he's almost stopped talking completely! I mean, the other day we went out for coffee. He'd just finished work – he works in a garage – and I was telling him about what happened in college that day. We got our exam papers back and Richie Hunk and I got the top marks! And when I finished I said, 'So, what d'you think of that then, Lewis?' and he said, 'What?' And so I said, 'You're not *listening* to me, Lewis!' – you know, quite firmly – and he just said, 'Sorry, Bella.' Sorry, Bella! That's all he could think of to say! And then when I was telling him about my art project – the college say I'm doing really well on it and they might put it on show to the public! Richie Hunk says it's great! – guess what? He turned away! He actually turned away! I couldn't believe it! 'Lewis,' I said, 'Lewis, if you aren't prepared to listen to me, I don't think I'm prepared to talk to you,' and I went straight home. I just can't understand why he's like this.

UNIT 21 B2

Bella's a lovely girl. She is. I've liked her ever since I first met her. All my mates say I'm dead lucky to have her as my girlfriend. Things don't always work out right when we go out. I ... I mean, I work really hard, and it's long hours – I'm a car mechanic, you know – so after work I'm often tired. Don't find it easy to say what I mean, either – never have. And Bella, well, she's at college, you see. She and her friends have an easy life there, so in the evenings she's full of energy – very lively and energetic she is. As you know, she does talk a lot. Tends to go on and on. I sometimes wish we could just sit quietly there together. To tell the truth, I quite often switch off. All those stories about what she's doing at college. I never had the chance to go, you see, and I wonder if one day she'll decide she'd rather be with one of her student friends than me. And if I hear any more about that Richie Hunk, I'll go mad! My mum doesn't like Bella much, thinks she's too proud of herself, so that doesn't make things any easier.

UNIT 21 C

Hello, Alexei, it's Luke here. Thanks for your last letter. You *are* lucky – you have a *normal* family. Wait till you hear about mine – they're all a bit mad!

I'll start with my dad. He works in a bank, but his big hobby is cooking and eating. As soon as he gets home, he rushes into the kitchen, puts on his apron and starts making some wonderful new dish. Huh! It all tastes the same to me!

Then there's my mum. She's a fitness fanatic and belongs to three sports clubs! We don't see much of her in the evenings because she's usually out jogging or playing tennis or doing aerobics. Not at the moment, though, because she broke her leg playing squash and has to walk with a stick for a few weeks!

My little sister Josie is *awful*! She *loves* school and studying and even homework! She hates sweets and TV and going out! Can you believe it? The worst thing is, she looks so silly when she goes out, because she always takes an umbrella with her, even if the sun's shining! She says she doesn't want to get wet!

Granny lives with us too. She says she's decided to enjoy herself now that she's over 80. So she gave up knitting and started doing parachuting at weekends. She hasn't broken anything yet.

My aunt, Auntie Joan, is even stranger. She lives just round the corner. Everything in her house is purple – walls, carpets, curtains – and she doesn't eat *any*thing till nine o'clock in the evening. Even her little dog Spot has to wait till then for his food. So you see how terrible my life is, Alexei. What can I do about my mad family?

Write soon, or send me a cassette.

Luke

UNIT 22 B

Well, I don't normally worry about money. But I did have a nasty experience once, when I had to be a bit careful. It was when my wife and I were on holiday, in a resort on the Italian Riviera. It happened to be her birthday, so I said I'd take her out to lunch, with a couple of friends of ours who we knew there. So, we walked along the beach and just stopped at a nice-looking place. The four of us ordered soup, and some starters, and fish, and steaks, and salad, and some wine, and sat in the sunshine enjoying all this. I wasn't at all worried about what it was going to cost, because I always pay by credit card if it's quite an expensive meal. But we were just about to order some fruit and ice-cream, when I put my hand in my pocket and found I hadn't got my card! I suddenly realised I was wearing the wrong trousers – I'd changed my usual pair because I'd spilt coffee on them at breakfast – and my card was in my trouser pocket back at the hotel! Huh. Well, this gave me a really horrible shock, and I tried to have a quick look at the menu while nobody was looking, so I could add up the bill so far. I had to pretend everything was OK – I didn't want to ruin my wife's birthday lunch by giving her something to worry about, and I felt embarrassed about mentioning it to our friends, who we didn't know all that well. I knew I'd got 180,000 lire in notes in my wallet – that was about £60 then – but we'd ordered some of the most expensive things on the menu, so I might not have enough. Ah, I just don't remember the rest of the meal. I really didn't enjoy it, because I was dreading the arrival of the bill. But when it came, I was so relieved! I had enough to pay it *and* leave a tip! I was cleaned out, had absolutely nothing left, but it didn't matter. What a relief, eh?

UNIT 22 C

Hello, is that the Midland Bank, the emergency help line? Oh good – look, this really *is* an emergency. The thing is, I've lost my card, my debit card, you know. At least I *think* I've lost it, but maybe it was stolen. Anyway, I haven't got it any more. So can you cancel it or something, you know, whatever? Then I won't have to pay if somebody else uses it – that's how it works, isn't it? You want some details, yes, right. I'm Victoria P. Brane, got that? Victoria like the queen or the station, OK? Then P for, well, I won't tell you what it's for, it's such a silly name! And then Brane, that's B.R.A.N.E. And the card number's 4989 1662 3972 1408. So is that it? You're going to cancel my card and send me a new one? Fine, thanks very much.

UNIT 23 B

The Clock Tower? Oh, that's very simple. You go up past the bank to the traffic lights, just by the roundabout. Go straight over, in other words take the fourth exit off the roundabout. You'll see MacBurgers on your left. You're now in Dyke Road. It should be straight on from there, but there are roadworks at the moment, you see. So just before you get to the church, on your right, and the children's hospital – the Royal Alexandra, it's called – you have to turn right into Clifton Road, then first left to get back onto the main road again. Then you go downhill to a big crossroads, and there's the Clock Tower. You can't miss it. So remember, it's straight across at the roundabout. If you go wrong there and turn off too soon, you'll end up at the station, and then you could just go straight down Queen's Road instead. But it's really busy round there at this time of day, so it's best to go down Dyke Road, as I said.

UNIT 23 C

1 My friend and I were driving around looking for our hotel in Seville, and it was really difficult because it's a one-way system and there's a very old part of the city, with tiny narrow streets, and a traffic policeman on duty at the ... at the sort of entrance to it. And anyway, we asked *him* the way, and he gaily waved us in the direction he thought, but it was no good at all, and in twenty minutes we were back again in the same place. He seemed a bit surprised to see us, and he asked his friend for help. They gave us a few more directions, so we tried again. And guess what? Ten minutes later we were there again, for the third time! The cops thought it was really funny, and we were all laughing like mad. Anyway, in the end one of them hopped on a motorbike and drove in front of us all the way to the hotel. Huh! We felt *so* important! I don't know, I ...

2 Well, this happened when I was in the States, years ago. I'd just arrived in some town. It was about midnight. I'd just got off the Greyhound bus I was on and asked the driver very politely, 'Could you tell me the way to the Sunnyside Hostel?' and he said, 'It's over there,' pointing across a car park. I could see the name lit up in the dark – it looked just a few minutes' walk away. But he also said, 'I don't advise you to walk across there at this time of night. Could be dangerous.' This worried me a bit, so I thanked him for his advice and went the long way round, out into the road. The trouble was, I couldn't see the hostel sign any more, and I didn't have a map, so I got completely lost. I was standing on the kerb wondering what to do next, when a police car drew up and a big policeman said, 'Hey, you shouldn't be walking around here on your own at this time of night!' I felt like adding, 'Could be dangerous!' But actually I was rather pleased to see a friendly face by then, and he very kindly gave me a lift to the hostel, so I never discovered how dangerous things really were in that little town. Just as well, really, because some of those ...

UNIT 24 B

1 Who? Claudia? Oh, she's very unsure of herself. Very nervous when it comes to exams and all that. Have you seen her lucky mascot? It's a key ring with a funny little plastic rabbit on it. She takes it everywhere with her for luck. She actually thinks things will be OK if she has it in her hand. Funny believing that sort of thing!

2 That's the boy next door, Jim his name is, very nice lad. He's studying at the moment and he just lives for his music. He's always carrying his violin around with him. Plays very well, actually, but I don't suppose it'll ever make him much money. He doesn't seem to care about that, though.

3 You know, old Miss Henderson's amazing. She cycles down the High Street, with every grey hair in place, and her shopping in the basket on the front. She's been doing it for years and has never had an accident, although the traffic's pretty bad in the centre of town.

4 You're talking about Gary, aren't you? Lovely clothes he wears. I think his mum's Italian, isn't she? And he always wears sunglasses! Makes him look cool, I suppose. He's always got the very latest T-shirt, or boots, or whatever. It's obviously important to him to look good.

5 He was my teacher in the first year, Mr Lewis was, really nice man. Used to tell us jokes sometimes. I understood maths when he explained it to me. When he left, I sort of lost interest. What a great teacher! None of the others were as good as ...

UNIT 24 C

1 Yes, Claudia's Scottish, actually – she comes from Dunbar, near Edinburgh. She's, oh, she's 16 now, I think. She comes from a large family, lots of brothers and sisters, but the funny thing is, she really finds it difficult to meet people, and *hates* going out. It's a pity really.

2 Jim's parents are both doctors, you know. The whole family are very musical, and they all play in concerts together. He's *such* a nice boy. Always says hello to you when he sees you, and even holds doors open! That's very unusual nowadays.

3 Apparently, poor old Miss Henderson had a boyfriend once, a long time ago. But do you know why she never got married? Because she had to look after her elderly mother, who was very ill at the time. So she gave up her freedom and her chance of getting married. I wonder if she ever looks back and thinks ...

4 Gary spends an awful lot of money on clothes. Luckily, he has a good job with a high salary – he works in his father's company. He certainly isn't mean. I know he spends money on his friends, too – buys them big presents on their birthdays, takes them out, that sort of thing.

5 Everyone at the local school liked Mr Lewis. He was a wonderful teacher. I feel rather sorry for him, now he's retired. He doesn't seem to have any hobbies, and he spends a lot of time on his own. I don't think he looks very happy. I sometimes think I should go round and ask ...

UNIT 25 B

1 It was always fairly quiet in our house because there was only one of me. I was an ... an only child, you know. My parents didn't like a lot of noise, anyway. They both worked from home. It was quite funny really – we all had our separate studies, and most evenings we'd go off to work in our own little rooms. I'd be doing my homework, of course. It was a pity I didn't have any brothers or sisters. I ... I remember being very lonely, really.

2 Well, we live in a huge house, really big. It's always a mess because there are six of us, although my mum and my auntie are always tidying up. My dad died when I was young, you see, so we live with my auntie and her children. They're twins and they're the same age as me, so it's great! They're just like my sisters.

3 At the moment I'm a student, living away from home. I live at my grandmother's. It's very convenient. Her house is only five minutes away from the university, so I can walk there and save on bus fares. We get on really well, and she cooks all my meals. She cooks better than my mother, actually!

4 My brothers are always telling me and my sister what to do because they're bigger than we are, but Dad says we mustn't argue and fight so much, now there's a new baby in the house. We do try to help Mum if we can. The thing I like doing most is taking the dog for a walk, straight after school.

UNIT 25 C

I'm very lucky really because, although I only have one brother, I have a lot of cousins and aunts and uncles. My mother is the eldest of ten children, so it's a very big family on her side. I won't even begin to explain who *they* all are, but I'll tell you about my father's side of the family.
My father, Joseph Brown, was one of four brothers. The eldest was Keith, my Uncle Keith, and he married Elsie down in London, and they had two daughters, Ruth and Helen, so those are two of my cousins.

My father was next, and then younger than him was my Uncle Arthur. Now, when Arthur was young he joined the Army and went off to India, where he married Kay, an Indian lady, and they had two sons, Jeff and Alan. Unfortunately, they got divorced – Arthur and Kay got divorced – and Arthur came back to England alone. So I have two cousins – two half-Indian cousins, in fact – that I've never met. All I know about them is that one of them – Jeff, I think – was a footballer at one time. So perhaps one day we'll actually meet up with each other. Anyway, when Arthur came back to England he settled in Blackpool and married Dorothy, but they didn't have any children.
And then the youngest of my father's brothers is my Uncle John, who lives here in Leyland, and he's the only one that's still alive. His wife was Kathleen, and they had two children as well, a son and a daughter, Stuart and Tina, so those are my other two cousins. So altogether, from my English side of the family, I've got six cousins: Stuart and Tina, Ruth and Helen, and Jeff and Alan.
Now my father himself married my mother Susan, who came to England from Ireland when she was seventeen to train as a nurse. They had two children, my brother Joseph and myself, Maria. There seems to be a family tradition of calling one of the sons Joseph, because my father's father was also Joseph.
Anyway, my brother Joseph went to study in the USA and he finally got married there. His wife is called Diana, and they have two daughters, my nieces Sarah and Alison, who are teenagers, and they all live in Seattle.

UNIT 25 D

1 He played tennis.
2 Does she watch television?
3 He runs so fast!
4 We cooked the meal.
5 She takes super photos.
6 We didn't pass Daniel on the way.
7 She washed her hair.
8 They write home every week.
9 He walked sadly away.
10 It looks like rain.

Sentences 1–10 are now repeated.

TAPESCRIPTS

UNIT 26 B

1 Well, I left school at 16, you know, and did a secretarial course. I'd always just wanted to work in an office, so I was really happy for a year or two. But then I realised how little money I was getting, compared with other people. I mean, secretaries hardly earn anything! So I decided to go back to college and in the end I became a primary teacher. Yes, I love it! I love working with small children.

2 I was a baker at first, you see, in my dad's bakery. I had to get up really early in the morning – that's when they bake all the bread. But I'd always had this thing about animals, you know. I really love animals, I always have done, and I began to think, well, why don't I retrain, as a vet? My dad wasn't pleased at all. He said, 'I'll buy you a dog if you're so keen on animals!' but that was no good, of course, and, er, in the end I did it. It took me over seven years to qualify, and I did all sorts of jobs to pay for it. I was a ... a window-cleaner one year, and then another year I was the ... the lifeguard at the local swimming pool. It was pretty hard, I can tell you, but worth it ...

3 Well, when my parents died, they left me the farm and I ran it on my own for about ten years. I don't know how I did it, looking back. A farmer's life is pretty hard, especially for a woman, even if you have help. Anyway, a few years ago, I just couldn't stand it any longer, and I sold the farm. I needed some time to myself, I wanted to relax a bit, I wanted to do my own thing. Now I just do a bit of gardening for people – they pay me enough to live on. I feel so much better these days, it's ...

4 I used to love being a firefighter, all that excitement and feeling you were really helping. I had some good mates I worked with, too. But I fell off a ladder, you see, and my back never really got better, so the doctors said I had to give it up. Sad, really. Selling fruit and veg isn't quite the same! We're the only greengrocer in the village though, so we do pretty well on the whole, can't complain ...

UNIT 26 C

People often ask, 'How did you learn all those languages?' but the thing is I lived in several different countries when I was growing up, and it just seemed natural to speak the language.
I was actually born in Manchester, in the UK, but my family moved very soon after that, and we lived in Paris for a while. My mother came from there, and she always spoke to me in French, from an early age. Later on we moved to Austria, for my father's work, and I spent long holidays in Italy with my sister, so my Italian is pretty good.
I went to university in Munich – that's a great city! – and then after graduating from there, I became a teacher. I started teaching French, German, Italian and English to private students. I really enjoyed it, and I think I was quite good at it, too. I remember my star pupil was an Italian count who lived in a palace! Well, not really a palace, but a huge villa, with servants and so on.
Anyway, after a bit I realised that being a teacher would never make me rich, and for some reason I thought that being a writer would! Crazy, eh? But I was right, as it turned out. I decided to write detective stories, thrillers, that sort of thing, and I just seemed to have a gift for it. I write a new one every year, and they've sold very well.
In 1990 I won the Silver Dagger award for the best crime writer of the year. I've now bought a fantastic house on the south coast of England, near Torquay, and that's where I live. I've always worked at home – I don't need an office or anything. It's all very simple, really ...

UNIT 26 D

1 when I was growing up
2 I was actually born in Manchester, in the UK
3 and we lived in Paris for a while
4 she always spoke to me in French
5 Later on we moved to Austria
6 I became a teacher
7 I started teaching French, German, Italian and English
8 who lived in a palace!
9 for some reason I thought that being a writer would!
10 In 1990 I won the Silver Dagger award
11 on the south coast of England, near Torquay
12 I've always worked at home

1 grown up, growing up
2 Chichester, Manchester
3 Harris, Paris
4 France, French
5 Austria, Australia
6 teacher, preacher
7 German, Germany
8 in a palace, Indianapolis

9 writer, lighter
10 1919, 1990
11 Turkey, Torquay
12 walked home, worked at home

UNIT 27 B

Good evening to you all. The outlook tonight looks pretty cold for some of us tomorrow, with a fair amount of snow here and there on higher ground, but some nice periods of sunshine to cheer us up in the coming week. I'll start with the south of the region, where Dumfries will be getting the best of the sunshine tomorrow, with maximum temperatures around 7° Celsius – that's above average for this time of year. Up in the east, Aberdeen will be in low cloud for much of the day, and Edinburgh will have fog for most of tomorrow. There'll be poor visibility on the roads in and out of Edinburgh, so watch out if you're driving. The Outer Hebrides, as usual, are getting the worst of the wet weather. Heavy rain will be sweeping in from the west tonight, so get those umbrellas out! Temperatures look low for Glasgow tomorrow, only about 2° Celsius at best. It'll feel really quite cold, so you may have to turn the heating up, or put on another woolly jumper! Further north, in and around Inverness, there'll be just a little rain, a few showers, and finally, further north still, up in the Orkney Islands, there'll be no rain or snow yet – that's on its way – but it'll be *very* windy. Better weather coming soon, but that's all from the Weather Room for the moment. Good night, and keep warm!

UNIT 27 C1

Betty: Hello, Grace, did you have a good holiday?
Grace: Oh hello, Betty. Yes, thank you, it was lovely for the first week. But after that, of course, the weather was simply terrible!
B: Oh dear, what a pity! It was very cold here, you know.
G: Was it? Well, in Florida – did you hear about it? – we had this awful tornado!
B: Oh yes, I saw it on the news! Oh, was there a lot of damage? Your hotel was all right, was it?
G: Well, no, we had to move out actually, to another hotel. I mean, it wasn't too bad, and nobody was hurt, and they were doing their best, but it was still very windy, and really quite cold, and there didn't seem to be any heating or anything.

B: Oh, I never realised. Poor you! Did it rain as well?
G: Oh yes – so of course we couldn't swim, or walk on the beach, or any of the things we wanted to do. Such a pity! Well, it's a relief to get home and get back to normal, I can tell you.
B: Well, we did have a little rain here last week, but on the whole it's been pretty dry, just very cold, you know ...

UNIT 27 C2

1 for the first week
2 hear about it?
3 this awful tornado
4 to another hotel
5 and nobody was hurt
6 really quite cold
7 Poor you!
8 things we wanted to do
9 Well, it's a relief
10 I can tell you
11 but on the whole
12 just very cold

UNIT 28 B

1 I come from Newcastle, up in the north-east of England, so I often do my training in the Scottish Highlands. There's usually quite good snow there. But at the moment I'm training in the Alps. It's cold and sunny, and the snow's just right for downhill skiing. I'm hoping I'll be in the team for the winter Olympics. That's the plan, anyway. I think I'll probably be good enough.

2 Oh, hockey's a simply *super* sport, a really good team game, you see. You can't just think about yourself and your own problems, you have to think about the *team*, that's really important. Out there in the fresh air, oh yes, it's wonderful! Of course, there isn't any money in it. It isn't a popular sport like football or even tennis, so most of us play it for love! Ha ha ha! In fact, my income comes from teaching it. I give lessons at a local school – the girls all love it there. But I'll be playing in the national team against Canada on Friday – pretty exciting, wouldn't you say?

3 Yeah, it's exhausting playing in a darts match, I can tell you. You need a bit of food to keep you going, that's what I say. I'll be playing for the Queen's Cup next month, and I'll be building myself up for that, eating well. Of course, the prize money goes soon enough, so to pay the bills I work as a delivery man for a furniture shop. Heavy work, but then, er, I've got the figure for it. I can pick up a piano, no trouble at all!

4 You can take a photo of me if you like. Everybody wants a photo of me. I don't know why. Must be because I'm so famous. Well, when you're the world's number one at snooker, it stands to reason, doesn't it? I'm making a TV programme about my life, and snooker, and then a bit more about me. Millions of people will want to watch it, because they find me interesting, you see? Still, now I'm world champion (did I mention that?), I don't really need the money any more. I've already got a Mercedes and a Ferrari – they're all right, nothing special. I think I'll probably retire from snooker soon. Doesn't seem much point in playing, really.

UNIT 28 C

Now this is very exciting. If you've just joined us, we're about to see what could be the final game in the final set of this match between the number one player, Lulu Bassett, and the almost unknown, up till today anyway, Rosie Finch. Both players are American. Lulu, the unbeaten world champion, is playing well but she looks a little tired, while the younger girl, Rosie, is still full of energy. And my money's on her. She's looking fit and fresh and her serve is pretty powerful, I can tell you. The players have won one set each so far, and this is the third and final set, which will decide the winner of the whole match. And at the moment Rosie Finch is in front, with 5 games to 4. She's in a strong position. This is the final set, remember, and it's Rosie Finch to serve.

The girls are ... are going out onto the court now. The crowd's clapping. It's a warm clear day in Los Angeles, and it's a great turnout. OK, the umpire's calling for quiet now, and here comes Rosie Finch to serve. Whoa, that was a fast one, and Lulu Bassett just couldn't get to it! One of Rosie's aces – a beautiful serve! OK – fifteen-love. Now Rosie's serving again ... it's in, and Lulu returns it, low the other side of the net, so Rosie has to run in to get

there, she's running, but, no, Rosie can't get to it. So it's fifteen all. The crowd's getting excited now. Rosie's mother and boyfriend are sitting in the front row, and I think I can see Lulu's husband and manager sitting just beside them. Rosie serves again, it's in, and Lulu hits it back, hard, and Rosie returns it. Lulu hits it into the net! Oh! Thirty-fifteen. Rosie must keep a cool head – she's only two points away from winning the world championship. She serves again, Lulu returns it but it goes into the net! Forty-fifteen, and match point for Rosie. Can she win this? She serves again. Oh that was fast! Was it in? Lulu couldn't return it, she's looking at the umpire, hoping it was out, but ... no, the umpire says it was in! Game, set and match to Rosie Finch, she's the new world champion!
Hah, the crowd's going mad! She's waving to her fans and running over to kiss her mother. But oh my goodness, Lulu's looking furious with the umpire! Lulu's husband's on his feet. Oh no, I can't believe this! He's just punched Rosie's boyfriend on the nose! Lulu's thrown her racquet at Rosie! It's chaos here at the Greenfield Lawn Tennis Club. Two paramedics are running onto the court – and this is Lee Mackenroe, in Los Angeles, returning you to the studio.

UNIT 28 D

child, children
man, men
woman, women
foot, feet
mouse, mice
tooth, teeth
leaf, leaves
knife, knives
life, lives
bus, buses
glass, glasses
beach, beaches

1	man	10	box
2	feet	11	house
3	tooth	12	potatoes
4	mice	13	hands
5	women	14	trees
6	child	15	breeze
7	prize	16	fax
8	dance	17	beach
9	cars	18	glasses

PRONUNCIATION BANK

A

1 hair, hair	5 live, live
2 were, were	6 said, said
3 boat, boat	7 idea, idea
4 chief, chief	8 later, later

B

please, pleasure
she, shell
cup, cupboard
fat, fatal
pot, potato
car, caravan
hop, hoping
plan, plant

C

walk
bird
thumb
calm
why
castle
cupboard
hour
write
leopard

These ten words are now repeated.

D

red, redo
rat, rate
own, gown
sit, site
bath, bathe
mat, mast
mad, made
hall, hallo
cost, coast
lose, loose
face, farce
hot, host

E

Delhi Durham Blenheim Birmingham
Minneapolis Seattle Montreal Reading
Edinburgh Peterborough Pittsburgh
Johannesburg
Leicester Worcester Gloucester Bicester
Bournemouth Houston Vancouver Melbourne
Salisbury Canterbury Newbury Shrewsbury
Brighton Kingston Wellington Washington
Norwich Greenwich Harwich Warwick
Yorkshire Cheshire Hampshire Shropshire

F

Argentina Japan Egypt Uruguay
Australia Europe the E.U. the U.S.A.
Dublin Paris Florence Geneva
Moscow Munich Berlin Madrid
Cambridge Manchester Glasgow London
Heathrow Airport Oxford Circus
the River Thames Trafalgar Square

G

tycoon marmalade yogurt pyjamas
yacht garage hotel karaoke
sauna mosquito carafe kiosk
chauffeur duvet siesta anorak
macho tattoo skiing bistro

KEY

UNIT 1

B1 Correct: 2, 4, 7, 8

B2 Owner: Mrs Jane Fletcher
No. of students: 40
Cost per student: £4 per night
What about beds? Sleeping space on floor
        "   washing facilities? Cold water
            only
Students must bring with them: Own food
    and a sleeping bag
No. of nights: 3
Dates: 17 – 19 July
Time of arrival: 3 p.m.
Total cost: £480
How to pay? By cheque
When? 6 weeks before

C1 1C 2B 3C 4B 5C 6A

C2
1 haven't even
2 we only need about
3 shall we start
4 who first stepped
5 mightn't they
6 no idea
7 actually
8 on a raft
9 remember him
10 I should think

UNIT 2

B1 1A 2C 3B 4A 5A

B2
1 From: Carol
About: seeing a film
Where: the Odeon
When: tonight
What time: 7.30
Where to meet: café in Market Street

2 From: Donald Ferguson
About: dinner with him and wife
Where: his house
When: Friday evening (next week)
What time: about 7
Dress: not formal

3 From: Jason
About: his party

Where: Jason's place
When: Saturday night
What time: 8
Address: Flat 7A

C1 1B 2A 3B 4B 5C 6B 7A 8C

C2
1 In a couple of weeks' time.
2 I'll do it straightaway.
3 I hope they can still fit us in.
4 How long's he been here?
5 We'll give him a good send-off.
6 That sounds great!

D
1 I'll <u>see</u> you to<u>mor</u>row.
2 She <u>posted</u> the <u>letter</u> last <u>night</u>.
3 The <u>present</u>? Oh, <u>give</u> it to him!
4 The piano was <u>sold</u> for a <u>hundred pounds</u>.
5 <u>When</u> does the <u>bank close</u>?
6 He'll <u>set</u> the <u>table</u> for you.
7 I <u>bought</u> a really <u>beautiful jacket</u> there.
8 Sit <u>down</u> and have a <u>cup</u> of <u>coffee</u>.

UNIT 3

B1 butter, carrots, cheese, chicken, courgettes, oil, onions, potatoes, tomatoes, yogurt

B2 1E 2A 3G 4D 5J 6B 7I 8F 9H 10C

C1 cream of mushroom soup, green salad, steak, chips, new potatoes, chocolate pudding, fresh fruit salad, wine, mineral water

C2 1 order 2 soup 3 please 4 mushroom
5 salad 6 steak 7 How 8 medium
9 potatoes 10 chocolate 11 fresh
12 healthier 13 drink 14 mineral

UNIT 4

B1 Number 1

B2 1 South 2 Central 3 train 4 call
5 0345 484950 6 your 7 following
8 update 9 into 10 suggestions
11 which 12 services 13 wish 14 renew

NATIONAL EXPRESS COACHES Monday to Friday		
BRIGHTON	**LONDON**	**BRIGHTON**
Dep 06.00	Arr *08.05*	
Dep *06.50*	Arr 08.40	
	Dep 08.45	Arr *10.35*
Dep *08.50*	Arr 10.40	
Dep every hour on the hour from *10.00*	Arr *1 hour 50 mins* later	
	Dep every hour on the *half hour* from 09.30	Arr 1 hour 50 mins later
Saturday and Sunday		
Dep *06.20*	Arr 08.10	
Dep every hour on the hour from *08.00*	Arr 1 hour 50 mins later	
	Dep every hour on the half hour from 10.30	Arr 1 hour 50 mins later
Fares		
<u>Single</u>	<u>Return</u>	<u>Day return</u>
Adult: £6	*£10*	£8
Student: *£4.50*	£7.50	£6
Child: *£3*	£5	£4
(Child=under 14 Dep=Departs Arr=Arrives)		

15 credit   16 any   17 connected   18 travel
19 select   20 want

C1
1 Brighton and London
2 Pool Valley and Victoria Coach Station
3 1 hour and 50 minutes
4 Yes
5 A child single – £3
6 0990 010104

C2 *See above.*

UNIT 5

A *Suggested answers:*
1 help us with our work, deliver leaflets, work in our shop
2 do overtime, get promotion, get to work earlier
3 look after yourself, eat well, phone home
4 meet tonight, go to a party, see you at the weekend
5 pay your membership fee, play in a match, help to organise a social event
6 change time of appointment, missed appointment, explain why

B1
1 About: a missed dentist's appointment
Number: 359821
2 Action to take: go to bed early tonight, ring her as soon as possible tomorrow
Number (mobile): 0976 360524

3 From: Jenny Smith
Action to take: see Jenny first thing on Monday morning
4 From: Edward Fowles
Number: 0181 748 1341

B2
1 Last Friday
2 She will have to pay the dentist £12.
3 Because Sylvia was very ill last winter.
4 Because Jenny is angry that Sylvia left work early again on Friday.
5 Help The Children
6 Working in their shop, delivering leaflets, collecting money

C1 1T 2F 3T 4F 5F 6T 7F 8F 9F

C2 1 relaxed   2 impatient   3 sorry
4 very worried

UNIT 6

A *Check the meanings of the words in a dictionary.*

B1 Sir Montague: in his bedroom, getting dressed for dinner
Charles: in the billiard room, practising billiards
Lucy Bisto: in the music room, playing the piano
Mrs Forbes: in the dining room, checking the table for dinner

Morgan: in Lady Paula's bedroom, discussing wines to have for dinner

Derek Donovan: in his bedroom, writing a letter

Morgan had the best opportunity because he was in Lady Paula's bedroom at the right time, and could have taken them while she was not looking. Derek Donovan and Sir Montague were also very near, in their bedrooms, and could have slipped into Lady Paula's room when they saw her go out.

B2
1 Derek wants to marry Lady Paula for her money, to pay his debts.
2 Morgan thinks Lady Paula will not be happy with Derek, who is only interested in her money, and life will be much easier for Morgan if Lady Paula does not remarry.
3 Sir Montague thinks his divorce from Lady Paula was all a misunderstanding and thinks they should get back together again.
4 He is jealous of Derek.
5 Lucy Bisto hates Lady Paula because she does not allow enough money to Charles, who Lucy is in love with.
6 Charles needs money urgently to pay his horse-racing and gambling debts.
7 Mrs Forbes has a son who is in trouble with the police.
8 Sir Montague might steal the diamonds, and accuse Derek of being the thief, so that Lady Paula changes her mind about marrying him. Morgan might do the same. Charles might steal the diamonds to pay his gambling debts. Derek might steal them to pay his own debts. Lucy might steal them because she hates Lady Paula and knows that Charles needs money.

The most likely thief is Morgan, who had the best opportunity and a good motive: he stole the diamonds so that Derek would be blamed and Lady Paula would break off her engagement, then life would be more comfortable for Morgan. He might keep the diamonds and sell them later – to buy a retirement home for himself and Mrs Forbes!

UNIT 7

B1 1B 2C 3F 4A 5D

B2 1B 2D 3G 4C 5A

C1 coffee, bread, meals, salt, tea, vitamins, fruit, vegetables, exercise, football, stress

C2 Correct: 5, 8, 9

UNIT 8

A The formal/informal pairs are:
I am extremely grateful./Thanks a lot.
I do apologise./Sorry I forgot …
Please accept this./Here, take this.
I hope you have an enjoyable time./Have fun!
How do you do?/Hi there!
My regards to your parents. Goodbye./Bye, see you later.

B1 1C 2H 3E 4G 5D

B2 1G 2E 3A 4C 5B

C1
1 Malay, Chinese, English
2 Malaysian
3 Chinese
4 German, Arabic
5 Malay
6 English
7 German, Arabic, English

C2 1D 2E 3B 4A 5F 6G 7C

D 1 6   2 9   3 9   4 9   5 7   6 17

UNIT 9

A 1D 2F 3B 4A 5C 6E

Travel agent's: 2, 3, 5
Check-in desk: 1, 4, 6

B1 1C 2D 3A 4F

B2 1T 2F 3F 4F 5F 6T 7F 8T

C1 1 32   2 10.22   3 15   4 11.05

C2	FLIGHT NUMBER	DESTINATION	DEPARTURE TIME	GATE	ADVICE
	BA2724	Stockholm	*10.20*	*29*	Boarding
	EAF3310	*Pisa*	10.22	32	Boarding
	AF8728	Riga	*12.15*	11	*Wait in lounge*
	KGC934	*Madrid*	11.05	*15*	Boarding
	MON692	Lisbon	11.10		*Wait in lounge*
	CA5541	*Athens*	11.25		Wait in lounge
	LH973	Bonn	*11.30*		Wait in lounge

UNIT 10

A 1F 2C 3B 4D 5A 6E

B1 theatre, play, matinee, performance, evening, prices, tickets, box office

B2 1 Company 2 Tuesday 3 Matinee
4 Thursday 5 7.45 6 £8 7 three
8 New 9 Wednesday 10 Saturday
11 £18 12 1 13 credit 14 box
15 348348

C1 Harry: C, F
Adam: A, E
Ellie: B, D

C2 1 OK, yes, why not?
2 Yes, that's a good one.
3 Who wants to be scared?
4 Maybe we should just go for a coffee instead.

UNIT 11

B1 1 The woman 2 The cost 3 The man – he is hoping to persuade her to rent the flat.

B2 Address? 30A Edward Road
Self-contained? Yes
Large? Yes
Warm? Yes
Any special advantages? (South-facing) balcony
How much per week? £100
Are bills included? No
Go and see it tonight? Yes
What time? 7.30ish/about 7.30

C1 living room, bathroom, kitchen, bedroom

C2 1B 2S 3G 4S 5B 6G 7S 8B

UNIT 12

A 1C 2B 3D 4E 5A

B1 1B, angry 2C, delighted 3A, worried

B2 1 problem, microwave, yesterday
2 happens, on
3 money, receipt
4 job
5 Paris
6 imagine
7 friends, 7
8 time, 10

C1 1B 2C 3D 4A

C2 1 tricky, idea, to lock it, push down
2 properly, getting started, first of all, on the keyboard
3 what I'd do, button here, disk in
4 really well, one end of the rubber, holding the handle

C3 1C 2D 3A 4B

UNIT 13

A A bread – baker's/supermarket
B meat – butcher's/supermarket
C stamps – post office/newsagent's
D vitamins – chemist's/supermarket
E newspaper – newsagent's/supermarket
F cauliflower – greengrocer's/supermarket
G dress – boutique/department store
H perfume – chemist's/department store/ supermarket

B1 bread, butter, cheese, tomatoes, cucumber, carrots, radishes, mayonnaise, chicken, eggs, tuna, olives, beef, pasta, salad dressing, white wine, fruit juice, strawberries

KEY

B2
1 what shall I put on my
2 What about
3 else do we
4 they're in the shops now

C1 1B 2A 3C 4A

C2 Correct: 3 and 4

UNIT 14

B1 This is the route that she took: New York–Washington DC–Atlanta–New Orleans–Los Angeles–Grand Canyon–Las Vegas–San Francisco–Kansas City–Chicago–New York

B2
1 25 years ago
2 To get to know American people/find out about American culture, to work and have a holiday at the same time.
3 Six weeks
4 By Greyhound/long-distance coach
5 New Orleans
6 In the corridor of a student hotel in New York
7 She thought he was in the UK/had no idea he was coming to the States.
8 He had almost no money.

C1 Correct: 1, 4, 5

C2 With Travel International company
Number of days: 10
Total cost: £3,000
Problems
Room: a) too small b) bathroom not cleaned every day
Food: a) too hot and spicy b) breakfast too small (just coffee and toast)
Service: terrible
Waiters: slow, rude
Excursions: a) no tour guide b) no lunch

UNIT 15

A A2 B4 C5 D3

B1 1T 2F 3F 4F 5T 6F 7F 8T 9F

B2
1 The woman: interested, sociable
   The man: in a hurry, friendly
2 The woman: in control, positive
   The new assistant: polite, unsure

3 First girl: surprised, sorry
   Second girl: angry, critical
4 The two men: relaxed, generous

C1 friend, jobs, leather, jackets, lab, scientist, chocolate, smell

C2 1C 2A 3B 4A 5C

D
1 Yes/I used to work with her actually/at Prada.
2 Oh really/what do you do?
3 Well/actually/I used to love chocolate.
4 Let me get you another drink/tomato juice was it?

UNIT 16

B1

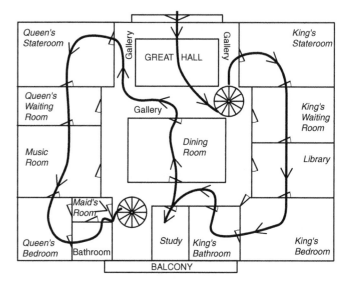

B2 1C 2B 3A 4B 5A 6C

C1 visit, boat trip, shopping, cost, cheap, bus, tea, restaurant

C2
1 go and see
2 feet hurt
3 a nice boat trip
4 enough time doing that
5 does it cost
6 pot of tea
7 I'm staying at
8 go to London

UNIT 17

A A sailing
 B rock climbing
 C driving fast cars
 D birdwatching
 E travelling

B1 1 Intensive French 2 Intensive Portuguese
 3 Intensive Russian 4 Intensive Japanese
 5 Writing Short Stories 6 Tennis
 7 Family History 8 Yoga
 9 Understanding the Internet
 10 Modern Art

B2 1F 2F 3F 4F 5T 6F 7F 8F 9T
 10F

C1 1 gym, £15 a month, 772438
 2 Body Matters, pool, 413992
 3 Fitness First, tennis courts, pool, £250 a
   year

C2 1B 2B 3C 4A

UNIT 18

A 1 capsize 2 yacht 3 deck 4 rough sea
 5 ferry 6 life-jacket

B1 1B 2D 3A 4C

B2 1T 2T 3F 4F 5F 6F 7F 8T

 The accident happened in the Irish Sea,
 between Larne and Stranraer, but closer to
 Larne.

C1 G, C, A, B, F

C2 1 … swim quietly away.
 2 … avoid it if you can.
 3 … go to hospital.
 4 … leave anything valuable lying around in
   your car.

D 1 been 2 thought 3 apple 4 five
 5 week 6 cottage, country 7 welcome
 8 writer 9 day 10 late

UNIT 19

B1 1C 2A 3B

B2 1 No, because Jessica asks what Amy's job is.
 2 She's a farm accountant/She helps farmers
   with their paperwork/accounts.

 3 Farmers are so busy that they don't have
   time for paperwork.
 4 She thinks it must be really lovely.
 5 She nearly had an accident on an icy road.
 6 She likes the fresh air and green fields, the
   open space and sense of freedom.

C1 1F 2T 3F 4T 5T 6F 7F

C2 1 have a nice weekend
 2 did you go
 3 it been open
 4 somewhere afterwards
 5 cost a bit
 6 do it more often

D UP: 12, 14, 17, 18, 20
 DOWN: 11, 13, 15, 16, 19

UNIT 20

B1 children, money, freedom, uniforms, lunches,
 pupils, stories, games, lessons

B2 1D 2F 3G 4B 5A

C1 Correct: 1, 3, 5

C2 1A 2C 3B 4C 5C

D Group 1 has the stress on the first syllable,
 Group 2 on the second syllable and Group 3
 on the last syllable.

UNIT 21

A modest/proud talkative/quiet cruel/kind
 energetic/tired nervous/relaxed

B1 1 two months
 2 the strong, silent type
 3 She and Richie Hunk got the top marks,
   and the college said they might put her
   project on show to the public.
 4 She thinks he doesn't talk enough, and
   doesn't listen to her.
 5 *Open answers*

B2 1 He's a car mechanic.
 2 Tired, because he's had a long, hard day's
   work.
 3 Energetic, because life is easier for her at
   college.
 4 a) say what he means
   b) talks

5 When she talks about college, because he's jealous of her/worried that she'll want to go out with someone else.

6 His mother, because she thinks Bella's too proud of herself.

C1 Dad D Mum C Josie A Granny E Auntie Joan B

He thinks his family are a bit mad, but it is not a real problem.

C2 1T 2F 3F 4T 5F 6F 7T 8T

UNIT 22

A account, bill, cash, coin, credit card, debit card, expensive, income, lend, menu (it has prices on it), pocket money, pounds, savings, tip, traveller's cheques

B1 1B 2D 3A 4C

B2 1C 2A 3B 4C 5B 6C

C1
1 The Midland Bank
2 A lost debit card
3 Victoria P. Brane
4 Cancel her card and send her a new one

C2 1C 2H 3K 4E 5I 6D 7L 8A 9G
10J 11B 12F

UNIT 23

A 1C 2A 3D 4B

B1
1	Clock Tower	8	church
2	bank	9	Royal Alexandra
3	traffic lights		Hospital
4	roundabout	10	Clifton Road
5	MacBurgers	11	crossroads
6	Dyke Road	12	station
7	roadworks		

B2

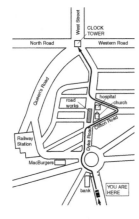

C1
1	In Seville	4	By (Greyhound) bus
2	By car	5	Sunnyside Hostel
3	Three times	6	Yes

The picture relates to the woman's story.

C2
1 Seville has a one-way system
2 he seemed a bit surprised
3 took them/escorted them/drove in front of them
4 she asked the driver for help
5 to walk across the car park in the dark
6 didn't have a map/couldn't see the hostel sign
7 told her she shouldn't walk around at night on her own
8 by policemen

UNIT 24

A shy/sociable sad/happy kind/cruel
mean/generous quiet/noisy polite/rude
unsure/confident unselfish/selfish

B1
1E (key ring)
2B (violin)
3C (bike)
4D (sunglasses)
5A (maths on blackboard)

B2 1E 2F 3B 4C 5G

C1
1 (1) near (2) 16 (3) large (4) difficult
  (5) going
2 (1) doctors (2) musical (3) concerts
  (4) 'Hello' (5) doors
3 (1) boyfriend (2) ago (3) married
  (4) mother (5) chance
4 (1) clothes (2) job (3) birthdays
5 (1) liked (2) wonderful (3) hobbies
  (4) own (5) happy

C2
1 shy
2 polite
3 unselfish/kind
4 generous/kind
5 sad

UNIT 25

B1 1C 2D 3A 4B

B2 1B 2A 3C 4A

C1

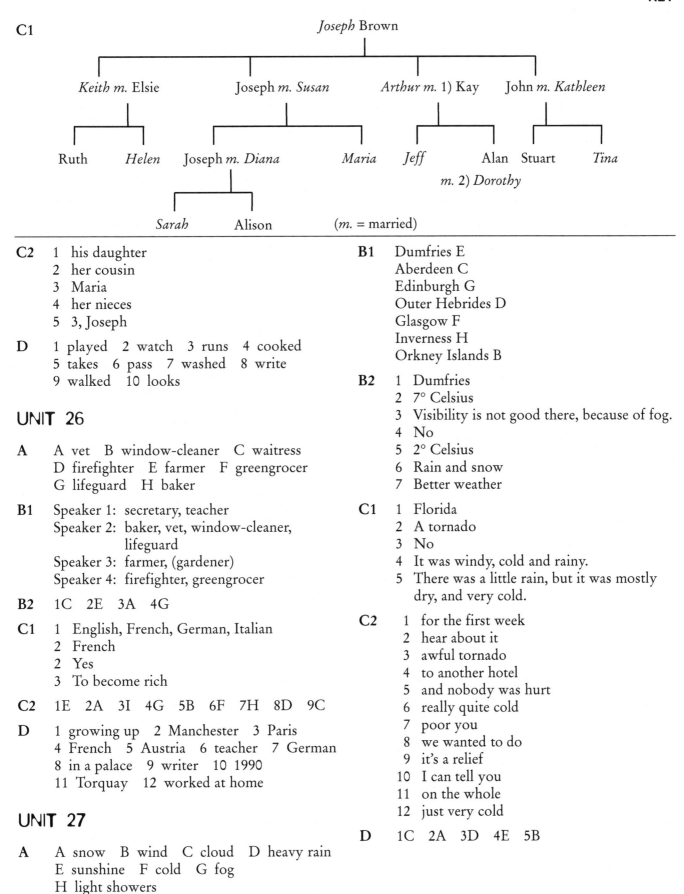

Joseph Brown

Keith *m.* Elsie — Joseph *m.* Susan — Arthur *m.* 1) Kay — John *m.* Kathleen

Ruth — Helen — Joseph *m.* Diana — Maria — Jeff — Alan — Stuart — Tina

m. 2) Dorothy

Sarah — Alison

(*m.* = married)

C2
1. his daughter
2. her cousin
3. Maria
4. her nieces
5. 3, Joseph

D
1. played 2. watch 3. runs 4. cooked
5. takes 6. pass 7. washed 8. write
9. walked 10. looks

UNIT 26

A   A vet B window-cleaner C waitress
D firefighter E farmer F greengrocer
G lifeguard H baker

B1   Speaker 1: secretary, teacher
Speaker 2: baker, vet, window-cleaner,
                  lifeguard
Speaker 3: farmer, (gardener)
Speaker 4: firefighter, greengrocer

B2   1C 2E 3A 4G

C1
1. English, French, German, Italian
2. French
2. Yes
3. To become rich

C2   1E 2A 3I 4G 5B 6F 7H 8D 9C

D
1 growing up 2 Manchester 3 Paris
4 French 5 Austria 6 teacher 7 German
8 in a palace 9 writer 10 1990
11 Torquay 12 worked at home

UNIT 27

A   A snow B wind C cloud D heavy rain
E sunshine F cold G fog
H light showers

B1   Dumfries E
Aberdeen C
Edinburgh G
Outer Hebrides D
Glasgow F
Inverness H
Orkney Islands B

B2
1. Dumfries
2. 7° Celsius
3. Visibility is not good there, because of fog.
4. No
5. 2° Celsius
6. Rain and snow
7. Better weather

C1
1. Florida
2. A tornado
3. No
4. It was windy, cold and rainy.
5. There was a little rain, but it was mostly dry, and very cold.

C2
1. for the first week
2. hear about it
3. awful tornado
4. to another hotel
5. and nobody was hurt
6. really quite cold
7. poor you
8. we wanted to do
9. it's a relief
10. I can tell you
11. on the whole
12. just very cold

D   1C 2A 3D 4E 5B

UNIT 28

A   A tennis   B hockey   C riding   D golf
E rugby   F skiing   G basketball
H baseball

B1   1   training, team
2   sport, money, football, income
3   match, cup, prize
4   champion

B2   1   downhill skiing, training in the Alps, be in
the national team for the winter Olympics
2   hockey, giving hockey lessons at a local
girls' school, play in the national team
against Canada on Friday
3   darts, working as a delivery man (for a
furniture shop), play for the Queen's Cup
next month
4   snooker, making a TV programme about
snooker and himself, retire from snooker

C1   They are all connected with tennis.
umpire: the judge or referee
love: zero
game, set, match: there are usually 6 games in
a set, and 3 (in women's tennis) or 5 sets in a
match
serve: to throw the ball up in the air and hit it

1   American
2   Rosie Finch
3   Because it's the final set of the world
championship match.
4   There's a fight between Lulu's and Rosie's
family and friends.

C2   1C   2C   3A   4D

D
1	man S	10	box S
2	feet P	11	house S
3	tooth S	12	potatoes P
4	mice P	13	hands P
5	women P	14	trees P
6	child S	15	breeze S
7	prize S	16	fax S
8	dance S	17	beach S
9	cars P	18	glasses P

PRONUNCIATION BANK

A   (The words heard on the tape are shown in
italics.)

1   A her   B here   C *hair*
2   A *were*   B war   C wear
3   A boot   B *boat*   C bought
4   A chef   B *chief*   C cheap
5   A leave   B life   C *live*
6   A sad   B *said*   C Z
7   A *idea*   B ideal   C I.D.
8   A letter   B lately   C *later*

C
walk: l	castle: t
bird: r	cupboard: p, r
thumb: b	hour: h, r
calm: l	write: w
why: h	leopard: o, r

Lightning Source UK Ltd.
Milton Keynes UK
UKOW07f2136191116

288021UK00022B/562/P